UNTETHERED

THE ART OF CREATING RESILIENCE FROM LIFE'S TOUGHEST MOMENTS

BRYCE GIVENS

INTRODUCTION

The metallic clang of the cell door echoes through the concrete corridor. It's 2 a.m. and I'm being processed into prison—strip-searched, fingerprinted, and issued my orange jumpsuit. Just three years earlier, I was a highly recruited offensive lineman for the University of Colorado, living what seemed like a charmed life. Now I'm watching a corrections officer catalog the few possessions I'm allowed to keep, wondering how my life unraveled so completely.

This isn't the story I thought I'd be telling. If you'd asked me back in high school, when I was fielding offers from top football programs across the country, I would have told you my future was set. I had the size, the talent, and the drive that coaches loved. My path seemed clear—college ball, then hopefully the NFL, maybe even a championship ring. Back then, I thought I knew what strength meant. I thought it was about being tough, pushing through pain, never showing weakness.

I was wrong.

Hi, I'm Bryce Givens, and if you're reading this, chances are you're no stranger to life's curveballs. Maybe you've felt the sting of failure, the weight of addiction, or the crushing pressure of expectations. Perhaps you're dealing with something less dramatic but equally challenging—the daily grind that slowly chips away at your spirit, leaving you wondering, "Is this all there is?"

I get it. I've been there. And let me tell you, it sucks.

The journey from star athlete to prison inmate isn't one you plan for. It happens in small steps, each one seems reasonable at the time—a painkiller prescription after an injury, the gradual increase in doses, the switch to harder stuff when the pills become too expensive or too hard to get. Before you know it, you're making decisions you never thought you'd make, crossing lines you swore you'd never cross.

But here's the thing: You're not alone. We're all struggling with something, whether it's a major life crisis or the slow burn of everyday stress. The problem is that we often feel like we should be able to handle it all on our own. We put on a brave face, push down our emotions, and soldier on, thinking that's what strength looks like.

Spoiler alert: It's not.

Real strength—the kind that lets you not just survive but thrive in the face of adversity—comes from something else entirely. It comes from resilience. And not the Instagram-quote version of resilience, with its empty platitudes about never giving up. I'm talking about real, gritty, hard-won resilience. The kind you build through failure, through pain, through hitting rock bottom and finding a way to push back up toward the light.

Now, I know what you might be thinking. "Resilience? Isn't that just a buzzword? Something people talk about but don't really understand?"

Trust me, I had the same skepticism. When I first heard about resilience in prison therapy sessions, I almost laughed. Here I was, a former Division I athlete who'd pushed through countless injuries, grueling practices, and brutal games—I thought I knew everything about being tough. But sitting in those concrete walls, stripped of everything that had once defined me, I discovered that everything I thought I knew about strength was wrong.

My journey from the depths of addiction to founding behavioral health businesses wasn't some Hollywood-style redemption story. It was messy, filled with setbacks, doubt, and moments where giving up seemed like the only sensible option. But through that process, I learned something profound about resilience—something that transformed not just my life, but the lives of countless others I've worked with since.

This book is about that transformation. But more importantly, it's about yours.

Because here's what I discovered: Resilience isn't some innate quality you either have or don't have. It's not about being tougher than everyone else or never feeling fear or doubt. Real resilience is about something far more powerful; it's about learning how to work with your fear, your pain, and your uncertainty, rather than against them.

Think about a bamboo tree in a storm. While mighty oaks might snap under the force of the wind, bamboo survives by bending. It's not about being unbreakable; it's about being flexible enough to withstand pressure without losing your foundation. This is the kind of resilience that saved my life, and it's the kind I want to share with you.

Through my work in behavioral health businesses, I've witnessed this transformation countless times. I've seen people come in broken, convinced they'll never recover from their failures, their addictions, their mistakes. And I've watched them discover reserves of strength they never knew they had. Not by becoming someone different, but by learning how to access and develop the resilience that was within them all along.

In this book, we'll break down exactly how that process works. No feel-good platitudes, no oversimplified solutions—just real, practical strategies backed by both science and hard-won experience. We'll explore the neuroscience behind why some approaches to building resilience work while others fail. We'll dive into specific techniques for developing mental toughness that goes beyond just "pushing through." And most importantly, we'll talk about how to make these changes stick, even when life throws its worst at you.

This isn't another self-help book full of empty promises. It's a practical guide born from the trenches of real struggle and transformation. Every principle, every strategy, every insight in these pages has been tested not just in my own journey, but in the lives of hundreds of people I've worked with.

What you'll find here is a roadmap for:

- Transforming setbacks into stepping stones for growth
- Building unshakeable mental toughness without losing your humanity
- Creating support systems that actually work
- Developing daily practices that build lasting resilience
- Learning how to trust yourself again after failure

Whether you're facing addiction, career challenges, relationship struggles, or just the grinding stress of daily life, the principles in this book can help you not just survive but thrive. Because that's what true resilience is about—not just bouncing back from adversity, but using it as fuel for growth.

So if you're ready to stop just surviving and start truly thriving, if you're tired of feeling knocked down by life's challenges and want to learn how to bounce back stronger than ever, if you're ready to discover what you're truly capable of—then let's begin this journey together.

You're stronger than you know. You have untapped reserves of resilience just waiting to be discovered. With the right tools and mindset, you can learn to face any challenge life throws your way with confidence, grace, and unshakeable strength.

Let me be clear about something: This journey isn't going to be easy. Real transformation never is. In my day-to-day work, I've seen too many people give up because they were expecting instant results or magical solutions. That's not what you'll find here.

What you'll find is a proven path forward—one that's been forged through real struggle and refined through years of practical application. You'll learn about the three core pillars of lasting resilience that I discovered through my own recovery and have since validated through working with hundreds of others:

1. First, there's Physical Resilience—not just about being fit or strong, but about understanding the profound connection between your body and mind. You'll learn how physical practices can anchor you during emotional storms and why movement is often the key to mental breakthroughs.
2. Then there's Mental Resilience—the ability to maintain clarity and purpose even when everything around you is chaos. This isn't about positive thinking or denying reality.

It's about developing the kind of mental toughness that
lets you face the truth without being broken by it.

3. Finally, there's what I call Spiritual Resilience—and no,
this isn't about religion. It's about finding meaning in your
struggles, about connecting to something larger than
yourself. It's what gets you out of bed in the morning
when motivation alone isn't enough.

These pillars didn't come from academic theory. They emerged
from the darkest moments of my life—from cold prison cells and
painful withdrawal, from failed businesses and broken relationships. They were forged in moments of crisis and refined through
years of working with others on their own journeys of recovery
and growth.

I've had the privilege of watching these principles transform lives
repeatedly. I've seen former addicts become mentors, watched
broken people rebuild themselves stronger than ever, and
witnessed countless moments of breakthrough as people discover
their own capacity for resilience.

That's why I wrote this book. Because every time I watch someone
break through their own limitations, every time I see that light of
possibility return to someone's eyes, I'm reminded of my own journey. I'm reminded that no matter how dark things seem, there's
always a path forward if you're willing to do the work.

1

THE RESILIENCE MYTH—BREAKING DOWN MISCONCEPTIONS

I can still feel the cold metal of that paddy wagon against my back, the bite of handcuffs around my wrists. I was being transported from Peer 1—a therapeutic community I'd been sentenced to—watching the world blur past through metal bars. That moment—that's when everything I thought I knew about being strong, about being resilient, finally crumbled.

The shame was overwhelming. Not just for where I was, but for everything I'd destroyed along the way—relationships shattered, potential wasted, a life derailed. I'd hit what they call rock bottom, but it felt more like a free fall with no end in sight.

But let me back up. Because to understand how wrong I'd gotten this whole concept of resilience—how wrong most of us have it— we need to start earlier.

Picture this: Texas Memorial Stadium, 102,000 people creating a wall of sound so deafening you can't hear your own thoughts. Our team is backed up on our own 15-yard line, down by a touchdown. The pressure is crushing, adrenaline surging through every player on the field. We've had to switch to a silent count because the roar of the crowd has swallowed every audible word.

At that moment, something shifted for me. My body was tense, my heart pounding so hard it felt like it might burst through my chest. But amid all that chaos, a strange calm settled over me. I realized then that being tough wasn't just about running through walls—just because I could didn't mean I had to. It wasn't about brute force; it was about precision, about being strategic.

Not that I listened to that insight. Instead, I kept pushing, kept forcing, and kept trying to be the toughest guy in every room. That's what society tells us resilience looks like, right? Look at the statistics: 52% of people report experiencing burnout. Among millennials, that number jumps to 59%. We're a generation raised on hustle culture, on "no pain, no gain," on the idea that if we're not grinding ourselves into dust, we're somehow failing.

I lived that mindset to its logical extreme. As a college football player, I was the embodiment of what society tells us resilience should look like. I pushed through the pain. I ignored warning signs. I was "tough."

And you know where that kind of toughness led me? Let me tell you what a day in active addiction really looks like.

You wake up sick—not regular sick, but a bone-deep illness that gnaws at every fiber of your being. Your first thought isn't about breakfast or checking your phone; it's about getting well, which means taking a hit of heroin. That initial rush brings a fleeting sense of normalcy like a weight being lifted off your chest, but you know it won't last.

From there, the day becomes a grind of chasing the next fix. You're constantly on the move—picking up more dope, selling to others, scoping out which seedy hotel to hole up in next. When you're dealing, staying in one place too long is a risk you can't afford. Every move feels like a drawn-out affair, and the meth makes you inefficient. Hours spent packing and driving, often in a fog of paranoia.

On days without dope, the anxiety is suffocating. The sickness creeps in like the worst flu you could imagine but magnified tenfold—muscle aches, cold sweats, vomiting, relentless nausea. Your thoughts race with dread: *Will I get the fix in time? Who can I call? What if I can't score?* The internal dialogue is a constant cycle of desperation, fear, and self-loathing.

That's what happens when you try to be "too tough to feel." When you push down every emotion, and ignore every warning sign, your body and mind find other ways to tell you something's wrong. Mine chose addiction.

It wasn't until prison that I started to understand what resilience really means. Every Sunday, this Buddhist teacher would drive three hours from Boulder to lead our meditation group. At first, I couldn't understand why anyone would make that kind of effort for a bunch of inmates. But he taught me something I'll never forget.

He talked about bamboo—how it bends with the wind but never breaks. Resilience, he explained, isn't about being rigid and unyielding; it's about learning to bend, adapt, and survive the storms of life without losing your core. That metaphor hit home. For the first time, I understood that I'd had it backward all along.

But understanding something intellectually is different from really learning it. My real education in resilience came in Peer 1, during what they call a confrontational group. Imagine sitting in the hot seat, surrounded by twelve of your peers, all of them looking straight at you, calling you out, challenging you to be honest with yourself and them. It's intense and raw, and there's nowhere to hide.

That's where I had to drop the mask. My heart was pounding, my hands shaking, and every instinct telling me to get up and walk out. But I stayed. And when I finally spoke my truth, it was like a weight lifted off my chest. I learned that vulnerability isn't weakness; it's the first step to real strength.

Walking meditation became my lifeline during those days. I'd pace the prison yard, focusing on every single step—the pressure shifting from my heel to the ball of my foot, the subtle crunch of gravel under my shoes. At first, my mind would race with thoughts of my past, my mistakes, and what the future might hold. But slowly, I learned to bring my attention back to the present moment, to the simple act of putting one foot in front of the other.

This wasn't the kind of resilience I'd been taught to value. There was no glory in it, no dramatic displays of toughness. Just the quiet discipline of showing up, of staying present, of learning to sit with discomfort without trying to numb it or run from it.

Let's talk about those myths about resilience that nearly destroyed me—and that might be destroying you too.

Myth #1: Resilient People Don't Feel Pain

I used to stand in the locker room after brutal games, my body screaming in pain, telling myself that acknowledging that pain meant I was weak. On the field, there wasn't room for deep, introspective thought. It was all about executing the job, playing every down with an edge, and out-competing the guy across from you.

But here's what happens when you try to be "too tough to feel pain": your body and mind find other ways to tell you something's wrong. The warning signs were there—the emotional burnout, the growing disconnect from people around me, the sleepless nights filled with racing thoughts. Physically, my body was telling me to stop. I was constantly exhausted, but I pushed through, ignoring the fatigue, the aches, and the creeping anxiety.

Myth #2: Resilience Means Going It Alone

"I got this."

Three words that nearly destroyed me. Three words I said countless times—to coaches, to family, to friends who tried to help. But in that confrontational group at Peer 1, surrounded by people who had been through their own battles, I finally realized I wasn't fooling anyone.

Breaking down in front of others, admitting I didn't have it all together—it was terrifying. My heart felt like it was going to explode in my chest, and I couldn't stop shaking. But instead of judgment, I was met with support. My peers didn't see me as weak; they saw me as human.

Myth #3: Resilience Is Something You Either Have or You Don't

This myth is particularly dangerous because it suggests that if you're struggling, it's because you're somehow deficient. I'd been that way my whole life—quick to learn, good grades, things came easily to me. On the surface, it looked like I had it all figured out, but deep down, I knew I didn't have it together.

But resilience isn't a fixed trait. It's a skill that can be developed, like building muscle in the gym. You don't walk in and immediately lift 300 pounds. You start where you are, and you build strength gradually, consistently, over time.

In recovery, I had to learn new ways of being resilient. The old tools—pushing through, ignoring pain, going it alone—weren't working anymore. They had never really worked; they'd just created the illusion of strength while making me weaker.

Real resilience, I learned, looks different.

Real resilience looks like awareness instead of avoidance. During my darkest moments in addiction, my internal dialogue was brutal. *You're worthless*, it would say. *You've ruined your life. There's no coming back from this.* It wasn't just negative; it was relentless, like a hammer pounding away at whatever little hope I had left.

There were moments when I would try to fight back, telling myself that maybe I could turn things around. But the doubts always crept in. *Why even try? You'll just mess it up again.* It was a vicious cycle of self-hate and despair. And the worst part was, I believed it. I believed every word of that inner voice until I hit rock bottom and realized that the only way to silence it was to change, to fight for a new narrative.

This is what real resilience looks like: not the absence of that negative self-talk, but the ability to recognize it, sit with it, and choose a different response. It's about being present with whatever's happening, even when—especially when—it's uncomfortable.

In my addiction, I was the master of avoidance. Uncomfortable feeling? Take a hit. Difficult conversation? Ghost. Personal responsibility? Run from it. I thought I was being strong by not dealing with things. In reality, I was becoming weaker every time I chose avoidance over awareness.

Real resilience looks like flexibility instead of rigidity. Remember that Buddhist teacher's lesson about bamboo? That wasn't just a nice metaphor. When you're deep into dealing, staying in one place too long is a risk you can't afford. But I was rigid in my thinking, stuck in patterns that were destroying me. Learning to bend—

to adapt, to change course when something wasn't working—was the real challenge.

This kind of flexibility shows up in three key ways:

1. First, there's emotional flexibility. In those confrontational groups at Peer 1, I had to learn to experience emotions without being consumed by them. When you're sitting in that hot seat, with twelve pairs of eyes on you, calling you out on your stuff, you can't run. You can't hide. You have to learn to feel everything—the shame, the fear, the anger— without letting it control you.
2. Then there's cognitive flexibility. During my football days, everything was black and white. Win or lose. Strong or weak. But life isn't that simple. Recovery taught me to see the shades of gray, to consider different perspectives, and to find new solutions when old ones weren't working.
3. Finally, there's behavioral flexibility. This was perhaps the hardest part. Changing how you think is one thing; changing how you act is another. Each step in my recovery required me to do things differently—to reach out instead of isolating, to face problems instead of avoiding them, and to sit with discomfort instead of trying to numb it.

Real resilience looks like connection instead of isolation. The World Health Organization estimates that depression and anxiety disorders cost the global economy $1 trillion per year in lost productivity (Chodavadia et al., 2023). Think about that number for a moment. That's the cost of our collective inability to connect, to reach out, and to admit when we're struggling.

In recovery, I learned that the strongest people aren't the ones who never need help; they're the ones who know how to ask for it.

Every Sunday, watching that Buddhist teacher make his three-hour drive to our prison meditation group, I learned something about commitment to others. In those confrontational groups at Peer I, watching people break down and build themselves back up, I learned something about the power of community.

This is what real resilience looks like. Not the highlight reel of triumph over adversity, but the daily practice of staying present, staying flexible, and staying connected. It's not about never falling; it's about learning how to get back up. And sometimes, getting back up means reaching for someone else's hand.

So how do we build this kind of resilience? Not the fake tough-guy resilience that nearly destroyed me, but real, sustainable resilience? Here's what's worked for me, and what I've seen work for countless others in recovery:

I. Start With Walking Meditation

During my time in prison, I discovered the power of walking meditation. It's simple but profound. You walk around, focusing on every single step. Feel your foot hit the ground—the pressure shifting from your heel to the ball of your foot. Notice the sounds beneath your feet. Your mind will wander—to your past, your future, your worries. That's normal. Just keep bringing your attention back to your steps.

I'm not going to lie—at first, it feels pointless. But here's what happens: You start developing the ability to stay present, even when your mind wants to run. You learn to observe your thoughts without being controlled by them. That's resilience in action.

I. Practice Brutal Honesty

In those confrontational groups at Peer 1, I learned that real strength comes from facing the truth about yourself. Try this: At the end of each day, ask yourself three questions:

- What did I avoid today?
- What truth am I afraid to face?
- What do I need that I'm not asking for?

Be ruthlessly honest with your answers. Remember, resilience isn't about being perfect; it's about being real.

1. Build Your Support System

Remember: Isolation is where the old thinking creeps back in. Make a list of three people you can be completely honest with. Not people who will just tell you what you want to hear, but people who will tell you what you need to hear. Reach out to one of them every day, even when—especially when—you don't want to.

1. Learn to Bend

When you face a challenge, ask yourself: Am I being rigid here? Is there another way to look at this? What would the bamboo do? Sometimes, resilience means completely changing your approach, even when it feels uncomfortable.

As we wrap up this chapter, I want to be clear about something: Building real resilience isn't comfortable. It's not about becoming some unshakeable force that nothing can touch; it's about becoming flexible enough to weather life's storms without breaking.

I still have days where I catch myself falling back into old patterns. Days where I want to isolate, to put on that mask of toughness, to pretend I've got it all figured out. But now I recognize those moments for what they are: opportunities to practice real resilience.

Before moving on to the next chapter, take a moment to reflect:

- What's your version of "I got this"—the lie you tell yourself and others when you're struggling?
- Where in your life are you being rigid when you need to be flexible?
- What would it look like to be truly resilient in your current challenges?

Remember, your journey to resilience won't look exactly like mine. But the principles are the same: Stay present. Stay flexible. Stay connected. And most importantly, stay real.

In the next chapter, we'll explore specific mental fitness exercises to strengthen these qualities. But for now, just sit with this new understanding of resilience. Let it challenge what you thought you knew about being strong. Because true resilience isn't about being tough enough to weather any storm; it's about being flexible enough to bend with the winds of life without losing your roots.

This is the kind of resilience that saved my life. And it's available to you too, if you're willing to unlearn everything you thought you knew about being strong.

2

MENTAL FITNESS—TRAINING YOUR MIND FOR RESILIENCE

The digital display on my watch reads 4:30 a.m.—it's pitch black outside, and every fiber of my being wants to stay in bed. But I'm lacing up my running shoes, preparing for another training session on my journey to the Ironman. This isn't just about physical conditioning; it's about something deeper.

You see, in those pre-dawn hours, when it's just me and the open road, I'm not just training my body; I'm peeling back layers, discovering who I really am beneath all the stories I've told myself over the years. Each mile is a conversation with myself, each step a chance to prove that I'm not the same person who once needed substances to face the day.

But let me tell you a secret about mental fitness that took me years to understand: Just like you can't walk into a gym and bench press 300 pounds on day one, you can't expect your mind to handle life's heaviest challenges without proper training.

The Power of Mental Rehearsal

I first discovered the true power of mental training in an unexpected place: therapy sessions. Now, I know what some of you might be thinking. Therapy? Isn't that just talking about your feelings? But here's what I learned: Therapy became my mental gym —a place where I could build the psychological strength I needed to face my past and reshape my future.

Picture this: There's a clearing in the woods from my childhood —a place where everything once felt simple and clear. During therapy, when memories would surface that felt too heavy to handle, I learned to visualize myself in that clearing. This wasn't about escaping reality; it was about creating a mental space where I could examine my experiences with precision and control.

Standing in that mental clearing, I could step outside my story and see it with fresh eyes. The memory that once felt like a tidal wave threatening to drown me became something I could observe, understand, and learn from. It was like having a control room for my own mind.

This technique—mental rehearsal—isn't just some feel-good therapy tool. Elite athletes have been using it for decades. Studies show that when athletes mentally rehearse their performance, they activate many of the same neural pathways as when they physically perform. The mind doesn't always distinguish between vivid visualization and actual experience.

But here's where it gets interesting: Mental rehearsal isn't just for athletes or therapy sessions. It's a tool you can use to build resilience in any area of your life.

Building Your Mental Gym

Let me share a practical exercise that evolved from my therapy experiences:

1. **Find your clearing:** Identify a place—real or imagined—where you feel centered and in control. It might be a childhood spot like mine, a beach at sunset, or simply your favorite room in your house.
2. **Create your mental workspace:** When facing a challenge, visualize yourself in this space. Make it vivid. What do you see? Hear? Feel? The more detailed your visualization, the more powerful the practice.
3. **Observe and direct:** From this mental vantage point, examine the challenge you're facing—not as something happening to you, but as something you're choosing to engage with.

This isn't about positive thinking or pretending everything's fine. It's about creating mental distance from your challenges so you can approach them strategically rather than reactively.

The Training Ground: Where Theory Meets Practice

Let me take you into a typical therapy session because this is where I really learned how visualization becomes more than just a mental exercise. I'm sitting there, and a memory surfaces—maybe it's from my dealing days, or a moment when I let down my family. Instead of letting that memory overwhelm me, I transport myself to that clearing in the woods.

In this mental space, I can actually see the memory like it's a movie playing out in front of me. The difference is that I'm not just reliving it; I'm observing it with purpose. I can notice details I missed before—maybe it's the desperation in my voice during a particular conversation, or the look in someone's eyes when I made a promise I knew I couldn't keep. These observations aren't about self-judgment; they're about understanding.

Here's what makes this practice powerful: You're not just visualizing a peaceful place to escape; you're creating a mental workspace where you can examine your experiences with the precision of a surgeon. This is how you turn painful memories into useful data.

Try this exercise:

1. Choose a recent challenging situation.
2. Find your mental workspace (your equivalent of my clearing).
3. Replay the scene, but this time notice:

- What were you feeling in your body?
- What thoughts were running through your mind?
- What assumptions were you making?
- What options did you miss at the moment?

This isn't about second-guessing yourself; it's about building a mental tool kit for future challenges.

The Ironman Mindset: Beyond Physical Endurance

Training for an Ironman taught me something crucial about mental fitness: It's not the big moments that define you; it's the small decisions you make when nobody's watching.

Picture this: It's 5:15 a.m. and I'm halfway through a training swim. The pool is quiet except for the rhythm of my strokes. My shoulders are burning, and my mind starts crafting perfectly reasonable excuses to cut the session short. This is where the real training happens.

Each stroke becomes a choice. Each lap is an opportunity to strengthen not just my body, but my resolve. I'm not just swimming; I'm practicing the art of continuing when everything inside me wants to stop.

This translates directly to mental fitness. Every day presents dozens of micro-moments where you can either strengthen or weaken your mental game:

- When your phone buzzes during focused work
- When someone cuts you off in traffic
- When a craving hits
- When an uncomfortable emotion surfaces

Each of these moments is your personal training ground. Like interval training for your mind, these moments build your capacity for resilience.

The Art of Cognitive Toughness

In prison, I learned that true strength isn't about being the toughest person in the yard; it's about being sharper than your environment. Buddhism became my framework—not just for surviving, but for thriving in a place designed to break you down.

Let me share what this looked like in practice. When anger or frustration would surge through me—and believe me, prison gives you plenty of reasons for both—I'd learned to pause. Not to suppress the emotion, but to observe it, understand it, and choose how to use it.

Think of it like this: Emotions are energy. Just like you can convert the force of a river into electricity, you can transform raw emotions into fuel for growth. But first, you need to build the dam—the mental infrastructure to channel that energy productively.

The Prison Laboratory: Buddhist Principles in Practice

In prison, I discovered that Buddhism isn't just a philosophy; it's a practical framework for mental toughness. Let me share a specific example of how this played out.

One day, another inmate deliberately provoked me. In the past, this would have been a straightforward equation: Disrespect equals retaliation. But now I had tools. Instead of reacting immediately, I observed the anger rising in my body—the heat in my chest, the tension in my jaw. I noticed the thoughts racing through my mind, the stories I was telling myself about respect and reputation.

This awareness created a gap between stimulus and response. In that gap, I found power—not the power to control others, but the power to control my own responses.

Here's a practice I developed from these experiences:

The Response Gap Training

1. **Identify Your Triggers**

- Make a list of situations that typically provoke an automatic response.
- Note your usual reaction pattern.

1. **Create Your Gap**

- When triggered, pause.
- Name the emotion you're feeling.
- Locate it in your body.
- Take three conscious breaths.
- Choose your response.

1. **Review and Refine**

- After each practice, note what worked.
- Adjust your approach based on the results.

This isn't about suppressing natural responses; it's about expanding your range of possible responses.

Small Challenges, Big Growth

Here's how to start building that infrastructure:

1. **Begin with micro-challenges:** During Ironman training, I didn't start with the full race distance. I started with getting up when the alarm went off at 4:30 a.m. Each small victory built confidence for bigger challenges.
2. **Practice purposeful discomfort:** Cold showers, fasting for short periods, or holding a plank for longer than comfortable—these aren't about punishment; they're about training your mind to function under stress.
3. **Use strategic self-talk:** When the voice in your head says "I can't," add "yet" to the end of that sentence. "I can't do this" becomes "I can't do this yet." It's a small change that opens up possibilities instead of closing them down.

Advanced Mental Fitness Techniques

As your mental fitness improves, you can start incorporating more advanced practices:

Scenario Training

Like athletes who visualize their performance under various conditions, start rehearsing challenging scenarios in increasing detail:

- What might go wrong?
- How would you ideally respond?
- What resources could you draw upon?

Emotional Complexity Training

Move beyond basic emotional awareness to understanding the layers of your emotional responses:

- Primary emotions (what you feel first)
- Secondary emotions (your reaction to the first emotion)
- Underlying needs and values

Integration Practices

Begin combining different mental fitness tools:

- Use visualization during physical training.
- Practice emotional awareness during social interactions.
- Apply Buddhist principles to daily decisions.

Remember, mental fitness isn't about reaching a destination; it's about continuing to expand your capabilities. Just like I discovered during Ironman training, there's always another level to reach, another aspect to refine, another challenge to face.

The goal isn't perfection. The goal is progression—one small choice at a time, one practice session after another, building the mental strength to handle whatever life throws your way.

Emotional Resilience: The Buddhist Way

Buddhism taught me something profound about emotional resilience: The goal isn't to eliminate emotions; it's to develop a relationship with them that serves you rather than controls you.

During those long hours in my prison cell, I learned to treat my emotions like weather patterns. Just as you wouldn't take a rainstorm personally, I learned not to take my emotional storms personally. They would come, and they would go. My job wasn't to fight them but to build a shelter strong enough to weather them.

The Three-Step Emotional Fitness Routine

Here's the daily practice I developed:

1. **Morning Check-In**

- Before your day starts, take five minutes to scan your emotional landscape.
- Notice what you're feeling without trying to change it.
- Set an intention for how you want to respond to challenges today.

1. **Throughout the Day**

- When emotions arise, use the "STOP" technique:
- Stop what you're doing.

- Take a breath.
- Observe the emotion in your body.
- Proceed mindfully.

1. **Evening Review**

- What triggered strong emotions today?
- How did you respond?
- What would you do differently next time?

This isn't about perfection; it's about practice. Some days you'll nail it, others you'll struggle. That's not just okay; it's part of the training.

Putting It All Together: The Mental Fitness Workout

Just like a good physical workout combines different types of training—strength, cardio, flexibility—a complete mental fitness routine needs multiple components. Here's how to combine everything we've discussed into a daily practice:

1. **Start With Visualization (10 minutes)**

- Use your mental clearing to rehearse challenging situations you might face.
- Practice seeing yourself responding with clarity and purpose.
- Don't just visualize success; visualize recovering from setbacks.

1. **Add Cognitive Training (throughout the day)**

- Set small, specific challenges for yourself.

- Practice reframing negative thoughts.
- Look for opportunities to step out of your comfort zone.

1. **End With Emotional Training (15 minutes)**

- Practice mindfulness meditation.
- Review your emotional responses.
- Plan adjustments for tomorrow.

Just like physical training, consistency matters more than intensity. It's better to practice for 10 minutes every day than for an hour once a week.

The Ultimate Test: Real-World Application

The true measure of mental fitness isn't how well you perform in controlled conditions; it's how you respond when life throws you curveballs.

During my Ironman training, there were plenty of days when conditions weren't perfect. Rain, wind, fatigue, doubt—they all tested my mental training. But here's what I learned: Those imperfect conditions were actually the perfect training ground for mental toughness.

The same principle applies to your daily life. Every challenge, every setback, every moment of doubt is an opportunity to train your mental fitness. Approach these moments not as obstacles to avoid but as opportunities to grow stronger.

From Training to Transformation

What makes mental fitness stick isn't just the daily practice; it's how these tools transform your entire approach to life's challenges. Think of it like learning to swim: at first, you focus on each individual movement. Eventually, these movements become natural, fluid, and integrated.

During those grueling Ironman training sessions, something profound happened. Those early morning hours weren't just about completing a workout anymore. Each session became a laboratory for self-discovery. I found myself connecting with raw inner strength, not competing for a podium spot (those elite athletes are insanely fast), but testing and proving my own capabilities with every stroke, pedal, and stride.

This same transformation happens with mental fitness. What starts as deliberate practice—the visualization exercises, the emotional regulation techniques, the cognitive training—evolves into something more organic. You begin to naturally pause before reacting. You instinctively create mental space when facing challenges. Your emotional responses become more measured and more intentional.

Looking Ahead: Building Long-Term Mental Strength

Before we move into the next chapter, take a moment to reflect:

- Which aspects of mental fitness feel most challenging to you right now?
- What small step could you take tomorrow to begin your training?
- Where in your life could you create space for regular mental practice?

Remember what I learned in that prison yard: Strength isn't about being tougher than your environment; it's about being sharper, more adaptable, and more strategically minded. Mental fitness gives you the tools to not just survive challenges but to grow through them.

In the next chapter, we'll explore how to maintain this mental strength over the long haul. Because building mental fitness is one thing while sustaining it through life's ups and downs is another challenge entirely. We'll dive into strategies for keeping your mental game strong when the initial motivation fades and life gets messy.

For now, start small. Choose one practice from this chapter. Maybe it's the morning visualization, the emotional check-ins, or the cognitive training exercises. Focus on that single practice until it becomes as natural as brushing your teeth. Build from there.

Mental fitness, like any form of strength, grows through consistent practice and patient progression. Your mind is ready to be trained. All you need to do is show up and put in the work.

Let's keep building.

3

LONG HAUL RESILIENCE— MAINTAINING MOTIVATION OVER TIME

E ight years.

That's how long my prison sentence was. Though I served only a portion of that time inside, even that fraction felt like an eternity. When you first hear a number like that, your mind can't really process it. It's too big, too overwhelming. The human brain isn't wired to comprehend that kind of time horizon. The days were slow, and it felt like time barely moved.

But here's what I learned: Whether it's serving time, recovering from addiction, training for an Ironman, or building a business, the principle is the same. Long-haul resilience isn't about heroic moments; it's about the small decisions you make every single day when nobody's watching.

Building the Foundation: Daily Rituals and Routines

Let me walk you through a typical day in my life now. I'm up early, focused entirely on training. Whether it's a long run, swim, or bike session, these workouts push me to new limits physically and mentally. After training, I shift fully to work in behavioral health businesses, dedicating time to my team and projects, ensuring I'm giving everything there.

Evenings? Those are sacred family time. I've learned to be fully present with my family, setting work and other thoughts aside so that each moment counts. This isn't just about time management; it's about energy management. Each part of my day gets my full attention, my complete focus.

The Power of Nonnegotiables

This structured routine requires more than just good scheduling —it demands unwavering commitment. In prison, I learned about nonnegotiables—those daily practices that you do no matter what. For me, it started with meditation. Every morning, without exception. It didn't matter if I was tired, stressed, or just not feeling it. This wasn't about motivation; it was about commitment.

Now, my nonnegotiables include:

- Morning training
- Meditation practice
- Recovery work
- Family time
- Service to others

These aren't just tasks on a to-do list; they're the scaffolding that supports everything else in my life. When things get hard—and they will get hard—these practices keep you anchored.

The Misogi Challenge: Pushing Beyond Limits

Once a year, I undertake what's called a Misogi challenge—an extremely demanding physical and mental challenge that pushes you far beyond your comfort zone. For example, I took on the 4x4x48 challenge, which involves running four miles every four hours for 48 hours straight. Imagine that—you're sleep-deprived, exhausted, and having to run again as soon as you've barely rested.

The Ironman itself was another Misogi. Training for months, then swimming 2.4 miles, biking 112 miles, and running a marathon all in one day—it taught me more about resilience and inner strength than almost anything else.

But here's what makes Misogi different from just another tough workout: It's not about proving how strong you are; it's about showing yourself that you're capable of far more than you think. These annual challenges aren't just about physical endurance; they're about mental grit and proving to myself that I can keep going, no matter how hard it gets.

The Marathon Mindset: Cultivating Long-Term Stamina

Training for an Ironman taught me something crucial about long-term resilience: It's all about pacing. You can't sprint a marathon, and you certainly can't sprint through life's biggest challenges. The race itself can be grueling, but I learned to break it down into manageable chunks—focusing on the next few miles, or even just the next minute when it gets really tough.

This same principle got me through my time in prison. Instead of watching the calendar and counting down endless days, I set daily goals. I exercised, read, meditated—anything that could give my day a purpose. The vision of who I wanted to become once I got out kept me grounded. Each day became about progress, however small.

The Process Over Progress Principle

When I first started training for the Ironman, I was obsessed with the finish line. However, I quickly learned that focusing too much on the end goal can be overwhelming. Life's challenges work the same way—whether it's recovery, difficult projects, or personal growth. It's not about sprinting through; it's about breaking big struggles into smaller steps, keeping a steady pace, and staying focused on the long game.

Instead of constantly counting down days or obsessing over the end result, I focused on:

- What can I learn today?
- How can I grow this week?
- Who can I help this month?

This shift from outcome to process thinking became the foundation of my resilience.

The Recovery Paradox

Here's something counterintuitive I discovered while training: Sometimes, the key to maintaining long-term stamina is knowing when to ease off. Just like in an Ironman, where pacing is everything, life requires you to manage both your physical and mental energy.

The paradox is this: Pushing too hard all the time actually makes you less resilient in the long run. True stamina comes from knowing when to push and when to rest. In training, recovery days are just as important as workout days. In recovery from addiction, understanding your limits and respecting them is crucial.

Finding Purpose Through Service

In my recovery journey, I discovered something powerful: Every struggle carries the seed of purpose. What started as a personal battle with addiction became something much bigger. I found purpose by showing up for others who are on a similar path. The process of getting sober wasn't just about my own improvement; it was about becoming a support for others.

I started to see my struggles as experiences that could help others find hope. What was once a source of shame became something I could share, and that gave meaning to the pain I went through. Recovery became about more than just staying sober; it was about inspiring others to believe they could overcome their own struggles too.

The Ripple Effect of Resilience

When you maintain resilience over the long haul, something interesting happens: Your journey starts to impact others. I see this every day. My own experiences—the failures, the comebacks, the daily disciplines—become tools to help others find their way.

This creates a powerful feedback loop:

- Your struggles become lessons for others.
- Their progress reinforces your commitment.
- The community grows stronger together.
- Individual resilience becomes collective resilience.

The Power of Community in Long-Term Resilience

Let's talk about motivation because this is where most people get it wrong. They think motivation is something you either have or don't have, like some kind of magical feeling that's supposed to carry you through tough times.

But here's the truth I've learned through recovery, Ironman training, and building behavioral health businesses: Motivation isn't a feeling; it's a practice, and it's deeply connected to the community you build around you.

In prison, I watched a pattern unfold that taught me everything about the role of community in resilience. There were always guys who tried to tough it out alone. They'd isolate themselves, convinced that strength meant handling everything on their own. Almost without fail, these were the ones who struggled the most, who often didn't make it.

Then others did something that, in prison culture, might seem counterintuitive—they built connections. They joined study groups, participated in programs, and formed workout crews. These were the ones who not only survived but often transformed their time inside into something meaningful.

I see the same pattern now in behavioral health businesses. Every day, I watch the delicate dance between independence and support play out. The residents who thrive aren't necessarily the ones who come in strongest; they're the ones who learn to balance self-reliance with the humility to lean on others when needed.

Think of it like training for an Ironman. Sure, there are plenty of solo training sessions—those early morning runs when it's just you and the road. But having training partners, coaches, and supporters doesn't just make the journey easier; it makes it possible. When I'm out on a hundred-mile bike ride, knowing I have training partners waiting at certain checkpoints keeps me going. Their presence isn't a crutch; it's rocket fuel for my own motivation.

This understanding shapes how I structure my own life now. My days follow a rhythm that might look rigid from the outside, but it's this very structure that creates the freedom to push boundaries and grow. Every morning starts in darkness, lacing up for training before the world wakes up. But even in these solitary moments, I'm connected to something larger—my training partners who'll meet me later, my family who supports these early departures, and the clients in my behavioral health businesses who draw inspiration from this dedication.

When I transition to work, it's not just about checking tasks off a list. It's about being fully present with my team, with our residents, and with each person who walks through our doors seeking change. Every interaction is an opportunity to both give and receive strength. I've learned that true resilience isn't just about building your own strength; it's about creating an ecosystem of support that lifts everyone higher.

Even my evening family time, which I keep sacred and distraction-free, feeds into this larger web of resilience. The strength I draw from these quiet moments with loved ones ripples out into everything else I do. It reminds me why I push so hard, why I maintain these practices, why I keep showing up day after day.

This brings me to something I call the Misogi mindset. While I take on major challenges annually—like the Ironman or the 4x4x48 challenge—the real work happens in the small challenges I embrace every month, every week, every day. Sometimes it's as simple as adding an extra mile to a training run, having a difficult conversation I've been avoiding, or sitting in silence a few minutes longer during meditation.

The key is understanding that resilience grows like compound interest. Each small action, each tiny victory, builds upon the last. Those extra few minutes of meditation gradually strengthen your mental control. Each workout, even the ones that feel insignificant, builds your physical foundation. Every interaction with others, whether giving or receiving support, reinforces your network of resilience.

The Spiral of Growth

I used to think of resilience as a straight line—you get stronger, better, tougher in a linear progression. But life has taught me it's more like a spiral. You often find yourself facing similar challenges but from different levels of awareness and strength.

Take my journey through recovery. Early on, facing a craving felt like being hit by a tsunami—overwhelming, all-consuming. Now, years later, I still occasionally face cravings, but I'm encountering them from a different perspective, with different tools, and with a deeper understanding of myself. The challenge isn't necessarily easier, but I'm engaging with it differently.

I see this spiral pattern play out in every aspect of my life. During Ironman training, I'll revisit the same tough sections of a course multiple times. Each pass brings its own struggles but also builds on the wisdom gained from previous attempts. In business, leading behavioral health businesses presents familiar challenges in new contexts. The fundamentals might be similar, but each iteration adds layers of understanding, new perspectives, and new ways to approach old problems.

The Daily Dance of Resilience

What I've come to understand is that sustaining resilience isn't about reaching some pinnacle where everything becomes easy. It's about developing a rhythm that carries you through both the smooth patches and the rough ones.

Every morning, as I move through my training session into meditation and then transition to work, I'm not just checking boxes. I'm reinforcing patterns that have become anchors in my life. When I'm fully present with my team, I'm not just managing a business;

I'm practicing the same principles of resilience that got me through prison, through recovery, through the darkest moments of my life.

The evening hours with my family aren't just downtime; they're active recovery, emotional refueling, and a reminder of what matters most. This daily rhythm creates a foundation that supports everything else. When challenges arise—and they always do—this foundation keeps me steady.

The Continuous Journey

Some days, everything flows. The training feels effortless, the work is meaningful, and the connections are deep. Other days test everything I've got. Like mile 20 of an Ironman marathon, when your body is screaming to stop and your mind is playing every trick it knows to get you to quit.

But here's what I've learned: Those harder days are actually the most valuable. They're where real growth happens. They're where you discover that resilience isn't about being invincible; it's about having the tools, mindset, and support system to keep moving forward, even when everything in you wants to stop.

It's like what I tell the members in my sober living business, Elevate Recovery Homes: You're not here to become someone who never struggles. You're here to become someone who knows how to handle the struggles when they come. Someone who understands that reaching out for help isn't weakness; it's wisdom. Someone who can turn their own challenges into strength that lifts others up.

As we move into the next chapter about relationships, remember this: The journey of resilience is both deeply personal and inherently collective. Every step you take forward creates ripples that affect others. Every hand you reach out to help someone else strengthens your own grip on recovery, on growth, on life itself.

The path continues to spiral upward. There will be familiar challenges and completely new ones. There will be victories and setbacks. But with each turn of the spiral, you're building something powerful—not just personal strength, but a resilience that radiates outward, touching lives you might never even know.

Keep moving forward. Keep reaching out. Keep building those daily practices that sustain you. Your journey isn't just about you anymore; it's about everyone your resilience will inspire along the way.

This is your path. Walk it with courage, with humility, and with the knowledge that you never walk alone.

4

RESILIENCE IN RELATIONSHIPS—
BUILDING SUPPORT NETWORKS

I remember sitting down with my family, my heart pounding in my chest, knowing what I needed to say but struggling to find the right words. Fresh into recovery, I had to have one of the most difficult conversations of my life. Not because it was confrontational, but because it required a level of honesty I wasn't used to.

"Look," I finally said, "You don't need to walk on eggshells around me. You don't need to hide your drinks or pretend things aren't what they are. I'm choosing to live this lifestyle, and that's my journey, not yours."

That conversation changed everything. Not just because of what was said, but because it marked the beginning of a new kind of relationship with my family—one built on honesty rather than pretense, on reality rather than wishful thinking.

The Foundation: Honest Connections

Here's something they don't tell you about resilience: It's not a solo sport. We like to think of resilient people as lone wolves, tough individuals who can handle anything life throws at them. But that's not how it works. Real resilience is built in relationship with others.

Research backs this up. Studies consistently show that people with strong social support systems are more resilient in the face of adversity. They recover faster from setbacks, handle stress better, and maintain better mental health overall (Ozbay et al., 2007). But here's the key: It's not just about having people around you; it's about having the right people around you and being real with them.

The science behind social support's impact on resilience is compelling. Studies at UCLA have shown that strong social connections actually reduce the production of stress hormones like cortisol, while increasing the production of oxytocin, often called the "bonding hormone." This biological response explains why people with robust support networks tend to handle stress more effectively (Taylor, 2011).

A landmark study published in the Journal of Clinical Psychology found that individuals in recovery who maintained strong social support systems were more likely to maintain long-term sobriety compared to those who attempted recovery in isolation (Islam et al., 2023). The research demonstrated that social support works through multiple pathways:

- **Stress Buffer Effect:** Social connections provide a cushion against life's challenges.
- **Direct Effect:** Regular positive interactions promote overall well-being.
- **Mediating Effect:** Support networks influence healthy behaviors and choices.

Understanding these pathways helps explain why building strong relationships isn't just emotionally satisfying; it's biologically essential for our resilience and recovery.

Building Trust Through Consistency

After prison, I faced a different kind of challenge. It wasn't about distance from my family; it was about showing them who I'd become. Words weren't going to cut it. Promises meant nothing. The only thing that would matter was consistent action, day after day.

Think about it: If someone has broken your trust repeatedly, would you believe their promises, or would you watch what they do? My family had every right to be skeptical. So I focused on the small things: being where I said I would be, doing what I said I would do, and showing up consistently. Each small action was a brick in rebuilding the foundation of trust that my addiction had destroyed.

The Power of Consistent Action

It wasn't dramatic. There were no big turning points or movie-worthy moments. Instead, it was about proving myself through a thousand tiny choices, day after day. Every morning I showed up for training. Every evening I came home when I said I would. Every commitment I made, I kept. Small things, maybe, but they add up. Each kept promise was another step toward rebuilding what was broken.

This is something I see now in behavioral health businesses: Trust isn't earned in grand gestures; it's built in small moments of reliability, in being who you say you are, consistently, over time. Each interaction, each kept promise, each honest conversation adds up to something stronger than any single grand gesture could create.

Social Network Theory provides fascinating insights into how relationships influence our behavior and resilience. Research has shown that behavioral changes—whether positive or negative—can spread through social networks up to three degrees of separation (Fowler & Christakis, 2008). This means your actions don't just affect your immediate connections, but potentially their connections' connections as well.

The concept of "social contagion" is particularly relevant in recovery settings. Studies by McGaffin et al. (2017) have found that:

- Recovery behaviors are 50% more likely to be maintained when supported by a strong social network.
- The optimal support network size for sustained recovery is between 8 and 15 close connections.
- "Weak ties" (acquaintances and casual friends) play a crucial role in providing diverse perspectives and opportunities.

These findings reinforce what many in recovery discover through experience: The journey to resilience is rarely walked alone, and the connections we build along the way shape not just our own path but the paths of countless others.

Strengthening Relationships Through Resilient Communication

The hardest conversations are often the most necessary ones. When you're in recovery, every interaction carries the weight of your past choices. However, I learned that avoiding these conversations only creates more distance. Instead, I had to lean into the discomfort.

That first conversation with my family about not tiptoeing around me set a precedent. It showed them that I could handle difficult truths, that I wasn't fragile, and that my recovery wasn't their responsibility. More importantly, it showed me that honesty, even when it's uncomfortable, builds stronger bonds than comfortable lies.

Attachment theory, pioneered by John Bowlby and Mary Ainsworth (Cherry, 2023), provides crucial insights into how our early relationships shape our ability to build and maintain supportive connections. Research (Sagone et al., 2023) shows that our attachment patterns influence:

- How we approach conflict resolution
- Our ability to trust and be vulnerable
- Our capacity for emotional regulation
- Our resilience in facing relationship challenges

The good news is that we can develop "earned secure attachment" through consistent, healthy relationships—even if our early experiences were challenging. This process involves:

1. Building self-awareness of attachment patterns
2. Practicing consistent, reliable behavior
3. Developing emotional literacy
4. Creating secure boundaries
5. Engaging in repair when relationships are strained

Using Conflict as a Tool for Growth

Conflict in relationships is inevitable. But what I've learned is that conflict isn't necessarily negative; it's an opportunity to deepen understanding and trust. When disagreements arise, the key is to:

- Stay focused on growth rather than blame.
- Listen to understand, not to defend.
- Take responsibility for your part.
- Use the conflict to build clearer boundaries and stronger connections.

Sometimes, though, even the most skillful conflict management isn't enough. When you consistently find yourself managing conflicts that arise from fundamental differences in values or life direction, it might be a sign that the relationship itself needs to be reevaluated. This leads to one of the most painful lessons I've learned about resilience: Sometimes building stronger relationships means ending others. Since prison, I've had to shed friend groups multiple times. Not because they were bad people, but because I was becoming someone different.

It's like trying to climb a mountain while carrying extra weight. Those old relationships, tied to old patterns and ways of thinking, were pulling me back down. Each time I had to make the choice: Stay connected and stagnate, or let go and grow.

Making the Hard Choices

Each decision to step away from a friendship group was harder than the last. It wasn't about judging them or claiming I was better. It was about recognizing that I was becoming someone different, and some relationships were tied to old patterns and ways of thinking that I'd outgrown. Each goodbye has made me more certain of who I am and the life I'm building.

This wasn't a one-time decision either. As I've continued to grow, I've had to reassess relationships multiple times. Each time, it's been about protecting my path forward rather than judging others' choices. Sometimes you have to make the hard choice between staying connected to old friends and staying true to your new path.

Setting Boundaries for Growth

Setting boundaries isn't about building walls; it's about creating healthy space for growth. After prison and through recovery, I had to learn that boundaries aren't selfish; they're essential for both parties in any relationship.

Here's what healthy boundaries look like in practice:

- Being clear about what behaviors you will and won't accept
- Communicating your needs without apologizing for them
- Recognizing when a relationship no longer serves your growth
- Taking action to protect your peace and progress

Cultural perspectives on social support and resilience vary significantly across societies. Research highlights important differences (Anjum & Aziz, 2024):

Collectivist Societies

- Emphasize interdependence and group harmony
- View support-seeking as natural and expected
- Often have built-in support systems through extended family
- May struggle with individual boundary-setting

Individualist Societies

- Value independence and self-reliance
- May view support-seeking as a sign of weakness
- Often require more intentional support network building
- Generally more comfortable with explicit boundaries

Understanding these cultural dimensions is crucial because:

- They influence how people seek and receive support.
- They affect boundary-setting approaches.
- They impact relationship expectations.
- They shape how resilience is understood and developed.

Recognizing these cultural differences allows us to approach relationship-building with greater awareness and sensitivity, helping us create support networks that honor both our cultural background and our personal needs for growth.

Recovering After Letting Go

When you cut ties with people who've been part of your life for years, there's a natural grieving process. It's okay to feel the loss while still knowing it's the right decision. The key is to:

- Fill the space with healthy relationships.
- Double down on your commitment to growth.
- Stay focused on building the life you want.
- Remember that loneliness is temporary, but compromise is permanent.

The science of social support reveals distinct categories, each serving unique functions in building resilience:

I. Emotional Support

- Provides validation and empathy
- Reduces anxiety and depression symptoms
- Increases sense of belonging
- Reduces cortisol levels

I. **Instrumental Support**

- Offers practical help and resources
- Reduces environmental stressors
- Provides tangible assistance
- Improves recovery outcomes

I. **Informational Support**

- Shares knowledge and guidance
- Helps with problem-solving
- Reduces uncertainty
- Improves decision-making quality

I. **Appraisal Support**

- Offers constructive feedback
- Helps with self-evaluation
- Provides perspective

Understanding these different types of support helps us intentionally build networks that can sustain us through any challenge. The most resilient individuals actively cultivate all four types, creating a comprehensive support system that can respond to different needs as they arise.

Building Your Support Network

Think of your support network like a building's foundation—it needs to be both strong and properly structured. In recovery and beyond, I've learned to build relationships in layers:

I. **The Core Group**

These are the people who know your whole story and support your growth unconditionally. For me, this started with family members who stuck with me through everything.

I. Growth Partners

These are the people who challenge you to be better. They might be mentors, colleagues, or friends who share your commitment to personal development.

I. The Community

This is your broader network of positive influences—recovery groups, professional connections, or others on similar journeys.

Sustaining Healthy Relationships

Let me tell you something that changed how I think about relationships. Through research and training, I learned that relationships don't actually maintain themselves in a steady state—they're either growing stronger or growing apart.

Research by Benson (2017) has found that successful long-term relationships share certain characteristics: Partners maintain a 5:1 ratio of positive to negative interactions, they make regular deposits in what he calls the "emotional bank account," and they practice what researchers term "active constructive responding"— showing genuine interest and engagement when their partner shares good news.

I see how this plays out in real time. Those small daily actions— showing up when promised, following through on commitments, expressing gratitude—really do build up what researchers call "relationship capital" that helps weather inevitable challenges.

Research (Stein, 2023) has identified key maintenance behaviors that keep relationships strong:

- **Assurance:** Regular expressions of commitment and care
- **Positivity:** Creating and sharing positive experiences
- **Openness:** Willingness to discuss thoughts and feelings
- **Task sharing:** Working together toward common goals
- **Social networks:** Maintaining connections with mutual friends and family

The science behind this is fascinating. Regular positive interactions with trusted others trigger the release of oxytocin, which strengthens emotional connections while reducing stress and anxiety. This creates a measurable biological response that reinforces positive relationship patterns.

What makes this particularly crucial in recovery is that we're often learning these skills while simultaneously unlearning old patterns. The research in neuroplasticity shows our brains can develop new relationship patterns at any age—we just need consistent practice and patience with the process.

Looking Ahead: Your Environment Shapes You

As we move into the next chapter about creating resilient environments, remember this: Your relationships are the most important part of your environment. The people you surround yourself with shape your thoughts, influence your decisions, and impact your growth.

Choose these relationships wisely. Nurture the ones that help you grow. Have the courage to let go of those that hold you back. And always remember that showing vulnerability isn't weakness; it's the foundation of genuine connection and lasting resilience.

The path forward isn't about isolation or independence. It's about building a network of relationships strong enough to support your growth while being strong enough to support others in return. This is how resilience spreads—not through individual achievement, but through the connections we build and maintain along the way.

Remember: You're not just building a support system; you're becoming part of one. Your resilience might be the inspiration someone else needs to find their own strength.

Let's move forward together, creating the environments that allow our relationships—and our resilience—to thrive.

5

ENVIRONMENTAL RESILIENCE— SHAPING YOUR SPACE FOR STRENGTH

In prison, your entire world shrinks to a cell. At first, this feels like the ultimate loss of freedom. But over time, I learned something profound: When you strip away everything external, you start to understand what really matters. Living with almost nothing, I discovered that most of what we think we need is just noise—distractions that often keep us from focusing on what's truly important.

That cell became my first lesson in environmental design. With such limited space and possessions, every item had to serve a purpose. Every square foot needed to contribute to either survival or growth. There was no room for excess, no space for things that didn't matter. This forced minimalism became my greatest teacher about the relationship between environment and resilience.

Science has now confirmed, through extensive research, what I learned through necessity. Our physical environment shapes not just our behavior but our very ability to think and process information. When we're surrounded by clutter and excess, our brains become overwhelmed with visual stimuli, making it harder to focus, make decisions, and maintain emotional balance.

The numbers are striking. People working in cluttered environments experience significantly higher levels of cortisol—the stress hormone that can interfere with clear thinking and emotional regulation. They struggle to maintain focus for extended periods, show decreased productivity on complex tasks, and even tend to make poorer dietary choices. It's not just about aesthetics or organization—our environment directly impacts our capacity for self-regulation, the very foundation of resilience.

The Daily Practice of Environmental Minimalism

Let me be specific about what this looks like in practice. In prison, I had maybe five books at a time, a few personal items, and basic toiletries. Everything had to earn its space. Now, living in a world of endless choices and constant consumption, I apply those same principles but by choice.

Think about this: The average adult makes around 35,000 decisions every day. Each item in our environment adds to this cognitive load—whether to keep it, where to put it, and how to use it. This mental energy is finite, and when it gets depleted, everything suffers: our decision-making, emotional control, ability to stick to healthy habits, and even our capacity to resist impulses.

Here's what this means in real terms: Every three months, I do a complete audit of my space. Anything that hasn't served a purpose in that time goes. This isn't just about physical items—it extends to commitments, relationships, and even digital spaces. The question isn't "Might I need this someday?" but rather "Is this serving my growth right now?"

This practice has profound effects on mental clarity. When your space is clear, your mind follows suit. It's like trying to run with a weighted vest versus running free—why carry the extra load if you don't have to?

The Power of Less: Creating Spaces That Serve You

The transition from prison's extreme minimalism to the outside world was jarring. Suddenly, I had choices again—about where to live, what to own, and how to structure my space. It would have been easy to fall into the trap of accumulating things, trying to make up for lost time. Instead, I made a conscious decision to maintain the clarity I'd found in constraint.

Research (Bolouki, 2022) has shown that our environment influences our behavior in powerful ways. Spaces that promote clarity and purpose share certain characteristics:

- **Intentional design:** Every element serves a specific function
- **Visual calm:** Reduced competing stimuli that drain mental energy
- **Natural elements:** Connection to light, nature, and natural materials
- **Functional flow:** Intuitive organization that supports daily activities

Since prison, I've maintained a minimalist approach to life, not because I have to, but because I've learned the value of it. It's not about deprivation; it's about intention. Every item in my space, every commitment in my schedule, and every relationship in my life needs to earn its place.

The Practice of Purposeful Spaces

I see daily how the environment affects recovery. When new residents arrive, they often bring chaos with them—not just in their minds, but in how they interact with their space. Their rooms might be disorganized, their schedules scattered, and their daily routines nonexistent. We start with the basics: creating order in their physical space.

Scientific research (Bolouki, 2022) has identified what makes a space truly "restorative"—capable of supporting recovery from mental fatigue and stress:

- **Psychological distance:** The environment helps create mental space from demands
- **Effortless attention:** Features that hold attention without requiring mental effort
- **Rich environment:** Enough depth and detail to keep the mind engaged
- **Supportive design:** Layout and features that align with intended activities

It's remarkable to watch the transformation. As their living spaces become more organized, their minds seem to follow. A made bed in the morning becomes a small victory that sets the tone for the day. A clean room becomes a sanctuary for clear thinking. These aren't just nice-to-have habits; they're foundational to building resilience.

The Digital Dimension: Finding Balance in a Connected World

When I got out of prison, the digital world felt like drinking from a fire hose. Social media, smartphones, constant connectivity—it was overwhelming. The world had accelerated while I was away, and I had to make a choice: dive in headfirst or be intentional about my reentry into the digital age.

The science behind digital overwhelm is fascinating. Our brains process digital information differently than real-world interactions. Every notification, every scroll, and every digital choice activates our reward centers in ways similar to addictive substances. This constant stimulation can:

- Disrupt our natural attention patterns
- Trigger stress responses
- Interfere with emotional regulation
- Create compulsive checking behaviors

I chose to stay completely off social media for several years. This wasn't about fear or avoidance; it was about understanding that after years of forced disconnection, I needed to rebuild my relationship with technology on my own terms.

The Clarity of Disconnection

During that digital detox period, I discovered something powerful: You can work on yourself and grow without needing external validation. Without the constant buzz of notifications and the endless scroll of others' highlight reels, I could focus on what mattered— real relationships, genuine progress, and authentic growth.

Research (Vanden et al., 2024) has shown that periods of digital disconnection can lead to:

- Improved sleep patterns
- Reduced anxiety levels
- Better emotional regulation
- Increased capacity for deep work

- Stronger face-to-face relationships

The silence created space for clarity. Instead of comparing my journey to others' carefully curated posts, I could focus on my own path. Instead of seeking likes and comments, I could seek genuine connection and growth.

Navigating Work Environments: A Journey of Discovery

My path through different work environments after prison reads like a story of exploration. Each new environment brought its own challenges and lessons about resilience. What I've learned about workspace psychology has proven invaluable in understanding how different environments affect our ability to thrive.

The Athletic Arena

Starting as a strength and conditioning coach at a baseball academy felt natural—it was familiar territory. The environment of discipline, physical achievement, and mentorship aligned with my values. The structured environment provided:

- Clear goals and metrics
- Immediate feedback loops
- Physical movement throughout the day
- Regular social interaction
- Tangible progress markers

But it was also safe, maybe too safe. I knew I needed to push myself beyond my comfort zone.

The Political Campaign Trail

Joining Bloomberg's presidential campaign team was a complete departure from anything I'd known before. Suddenly, I was in an environment of rapid changes, high stakes, and complex team dynamics. This high-pressure environment taught me about:

- Adapting to constant change
- Managing multiple priorities
- Building resilience under pressure
- Navigating complex social structures
- Making decisions with limited information

It taught me that resilience isn't just about personal strength; it's about adapting to and thriving in completely new contexts.

The Entrepreneurial Experiments

Then came the ventures into business ownership. The ghost kitchen pizza place seemed like a good idea—low overhead, growing market. The athlete-focused food prep service aligned with my background in sports. Neither lasted long, but both taught me invaluable lessons about resilience in the face of failure.

These experiences revealed crucial insights about work environments:

- The importance of alignment between values and space
- How the environment affects decision-making quality
- The role of physical space in mental clarity
- The impact of isolation versus connection
- The relationship between environment and innovation

Learning Through Business Evolution

The ghost kitchen taught me something crucial about the environment: Sometimes what looks good on paper doesn't feel right in practice. The isolated nature of the work, the lack of direct customer interaction, the sterile environment—it all felt disconnected from the kind of impact I wanted to make. The athlete meal prep service was closer to my passion, but still wasn't quite right.

Environmental psychology shows us that our workspaces need to support:

- Our core values and mission
- Natural human interaction patterns
- Physical and mental well-being
- Creative problem-solving
- Sustainable energy management

These "failures" weren't really failures at all. They were environmental experiments, each one helping me understand better what kind of space I needed to thrive. Every closed business was a step closer to finding my true path in the recovery industry.

Creating Resilient Work Spaces

In behavioral health businesses, everything I learned about environments came together. Here, we're not just running a business; we're creating an ecosystem of recovery and growth. Every aspect of our environment is designed with purpose:

Physical Design for Mental Clarity

The layout of our spaces encourages both community and personal reflection. Common areas foster connection and support, while private spaces allow for the individual work of recovery. Research shows that effective recovery environments need:

1. **Light and Nature**

- Natural lighting that supports circadian rhythms
- Views of nature that reduce stress
- Plants and natural materials that improve air quality
- Outdoor spaces for movement and reflection

1. **Sound Design**

- Quiet spaces for focused work
- Social areas for connection
- Natural sound elements for stress reduction
- Acoustic barriers for privacy

1. **Color and Texture**

- Calming color schemes that support focus
- Varied textures for sensory engagement
- Clean lines for visual clarity
- Comfortable materials for physical ease

This balance didn't happen by accident—it came from understanding how the environment shapes behavior and mindset.

Structured Freedom

One of the most important lessons from prison was about the value of structured time. In our recovery homes, we create daily routines that provide structure without feeling restrictive. It's about finding the sweet spot between too much freedom (which can be overwhelming for someone in early recovery) and too much control (which can prevent genuine growth).

The Digital Balance in Recovery

Today, I have a different relationship with technology than during my initial digital detox. I've learned to use digital tools purposefully while maintaining healthy boundaries. At Elevate Recovery Homes, we teach residents to develop what researchers call "digital wellness"—a balanced approach to technology that supports rather than hinders recovery.

This includes:

- Creating intentional usage patterns
- Setting clear boundaries around technology
- Using digital tools for connection rather than escape
- Maintaining real-world relationships as primary
- Developing a healthy online-offline balance

The Environmental Ripple Effect

One of the most powerful things I've learned is how changes in the environment create ripple effects through every aspect of life. When we help someone in our businesses organize their living space, we often see improvements in their:

- Mental clarity and focus
- Emotional regulation
- Relationship quality
- Recovery progress
- Overall sense of purpose

This isn't a coincidence. Your environment is either working for you or against you at every moment.

Building Forward: Your Next Steps

As we look ahead to the next chapter on mental dialogue, remember that your environment is the stage on which all other changes play out. The clearer and more supportive your environment, the easier it becomes to maintain positive mental patterns.

Start with one small change. Maybe it's clearing out a closet, redesigning your workspace, or establishing a morning routine. Let that change settle, observe its effects, and then build on it.

Remember: You're not just creating spaces; you're creating possibilities. Every environmental choice you make is setting the stage for your future growth and resilience.

Your space shapes your reality. Make it count.

In the next chapter, we'll explore how to develop the mental dialogue that complements these environmental changes. Because when your outer world and inner world align, that's when true resilience flourishes.

This isn't about creating perfect spaces; it's about creating spaces that perfect you.

6

THE RESILIENT MINDSET—SHIFTING YOUR INTERNAL DIALOGUE

B efore I share my story, let's understand why our thoughts have such profound power over our lives. Our brains process about 60,000 thoughts per day, and research shows that for most people, 80% of these thoughts are negative (Sun, 2023). This isn't because we're naturally pessimistic—it's a survival mechanism built into our neural architecture over millions of years of evolution. Our ancestors needed to be hyper-vigilant about threats to survive, and this vigilance is still hard-wired into our brains today.

Understanding this biological foundation helps us realize that negative thought patterns aren't a personal failure; they're a natural tendency we all must learn to manage. The key difference between those who thrive and those who struggle often isn't the number of negative thoughts they have, but how they process and respond to them.

When we repeatedly think certain thoughts, we strengthen neural pathways in our brains—it's like wearing a path through a field by walking the same route every day. This process, called neuroplasticity, means our thought patterns become more automatic over time. The good news is that this same mechanism allows us to create new, more empowering patterns through conscious effort and repetition.

This understanding of how our brains work set the stage for my own journey of transformation. Let me share how I put these principles into practice in one of the most challenging moments of my life...

I remember standing in front of the mirror shortly after getting out of prison. The reflection staring back at me told a story of failure—years lost to addiction, poor decisions, wasted potential. But at that moment, I made a choice that would change everything. Instead of seeing someone who'd lost years to addiction and bad decisions, I forced myself to see something different: *This is the guy who survived all that, who's still here, and who's going to build something from it.*

That mirror moment wasn't just about positive thinking; it was about taking control of my internal dialogue. The voice in your head either builds you up or tears you down. There's no neutral ground. Every thought either moves you forward or holds you back.

The Power of Reframing

Let me break down what reframing actually means because it's not about sugarcoating reality or pretending everything's fine. During those early days after prison, my mind would often default to thoughts like: *Who's going to hire someone with a record? I've wasted too many years. I'll never make up for lost time.*

What happens in our brains during these moments is fascinating. When we have a negative thought, it activates our amygdala—the brain's threat detection center. This triggers a cascade of stress hormones that can cloud our judgment and reinforce negative thinking patterns. But here's the amazing thing: When we consciously reframe a situation, we can actually redirect neural pathways, engaging our prefrontal cortex—the part of our brain responsible for rational thinking and problem-solving.

These weren't just thoughts; they were stories I was telling myself about who I was and what was possible. The key to reframing wasn't to ignore these thoughts but to challenge them: "Who's going to hire someone with a record?" became "Who's going to benefit from someone who's learned from their mistakes?" "I've wasted too many years," transformed into "I have experiences that can help others avoid the same pitfalls." "I'll never make up for lost time," shifted to "Every day forward is a chance to create something meaningful."

This process of reframing follows a specific pattern:

1. Recognize the negative thought pattern.
2. Pause and create space between thought and reaction.
3. Question the underlying assumptions.
4. Generate alternative perspectives.
5. Choose a more empowering interpretation.

The Daily Battle of Internal Dialogue

Before we dive deeper into my story, it's crucial to understand the science behind cognitive restructuring—the formal term for what I was doing intuitively. This process involves several key components:

- **Metacognition:** The ability to think about your thinking
- **Pattern recognition:** Identifying recurring thought patterns and triggers

- **Cognitive flexibility:** The capacity to consider alternative perspectives
- **Executive function:** The mental skills that help you execute new thought patterns

When we engage in cognitive restructuring, we're not just trying to "think positive." We're actually rewiring our brain's default response patterns. This process involves the activation of multiple brain regions, particularly the prefrontal cortex, which is responsible for higher-order thinking and emotional regulation.

Prison wasn't just a place I left; it became an experience I could transform. Every morning, I had to consciously choose which lens I would view my life through. The easy path was to see myself as an ex-con, someone marked by their past. The resilient path was to see myself as someone who had survived extreme challenges and gained unique insights that could serve others.

This wasn't easy. Your mind wants to fall back into familiar patterns, especially when you're stressed or tired. When doubt crept in—and it crept in often—I had to consciously redirect my thoughts. It wasn't about denying the reality of my past; it was about choosing how that past would shape my future.

The Growth Mindset Revolution

I'll never forget my first job interview after getting out. Walking in, I could feel the weight of my record hanging over me. Every instinct told me to hide it, to downplay it, to apologize for it. Instead, I chose to reframe it entirely.

Instead of seeing myself as a guy with a prison record, I chose to see myself as someone who had overcome serious challenges and could bring that resilience to the workplace. This wasn't just positive thinking; it was a strategic decision to transform what many would see as a liability into an asset.

The Science of Resilience

Recent research (Manjula & Srivastava, 2022) in psychological resilience has identified several key components that determine how well people bounce back from adversity:

- **Emotional regulation:** The ability to manage strong emotions
- **Impulse control:** The capacity to resist immediate gratification
- **Causal analysis:** The skill of accurately identifying the causes of problems
- **Self-efficacy:** The belief in one's ability to handle challenges
- **Realistic optimism:** The ability to maintain hope while acknowledging reality
- **Empathy:** The capacity to understand and connect with others
- **Reaching out:** The willingness to take on new challenges and opportunities

Understanding these components helped me realize that resilience isn't just about "toughing it out." It's about developing specific psychological skills that can be learned and strengthened over time.

From Liability to Asset

During the interview, I focused on what I'd learned and how those lessons could add value. I talked about understanding consequences, taking responsibility, and the discipline learned through adversity. To my surprise, they respected my honesty and drive, and I landed the job.

That experience taught me something crucial about the power of mindset: People don't just respond to your past; they respond to how you carry it. From that point on, I knew I could build something new if I kept learning, adapting, and seeing every challenge as a chance to grow.

The Psychology of Transformation

The process of personal transformation involves several distinct psychological phases:

1. **Discontinuity:** The moment when old patterns become unsustainable
2. **Disorientation:** The uncomfortable period of letting go of old identities
3. **Reorientation:** The phase of exploring new possibilities
4. **Integration:** The process of embodying new patterns and beliefs

Understanding these phases helped me recognize that the discomfort I was feeling wasn't a sign of failure; it was a natural part of the transformation process.

The Architecture of Mental Toughness

Think of your mind like any other muscle. When you first start working out, you can't lift heavy weights. You start small, build proper form, and gradually increase the load. The same principle applies to mental resilience.

Each day presents dozens of opportunities to strengthen your mental game:

- When someone questions your past
- When old environments trigger old thoughts
- When failure tempts you to fall back into negative patterns
- When success challenges you to maintain humility and hunger

The Role of Social Connection in Mental Resilience

One aspect of mental toughness that often gets overlooked is the role of social connection. While much of our focus is on individual mindset and personal practices, research (Li et al., 2021) shows that social support is crucial for building and maintaining mental resilience. This involves:

- Having people who believe in you when you doubt yourself
- Finding mentors who have walked similar paths
- Building a network that supports your growth
- Creating opportunities to help others, which reinforces your own progress

In my case, starting my behavioral health business wasn't just about providing housing; it was about creating a community where people could support each other's mental and emotional growth.

The Practice of Productive Discomfort

Instead of avoiding difficult situations, I learned to lean into them.

Each uncomfortable moment became an opportunity to strengthen my mental resilience. Whether it was:

- Explaining my background to potential business partners
- Facing old environments without old coping mechanisms
- Making amends with people I'd hurt
- Starting over when business ventures failed

Every challenge became a rep in my mental gym.

Building Your Mental Tool Kit

Let me break down what this actually looks like in practice. It's one thing to talk about mental toughness, it's another to build it systematically, day by day. Here's how I approached it:

Morning Mental Prep

Before anything else each day, I take time to set my mental foundation. This isn't about pumping myself up with motivational quotes or denying the challenges ahead. It's about grounding myself in reality while maintaining an empowered perspective.

When I was first starting my recovery home business, Elevate Recovery Homes, each morning brought a new set of potential obstacles: funding challenges, regulatory hurdles, and skepticism from others. Instead of letting these challenges overwhelm me first thing in the morning, I learned to process them differently:

- **Challenge:** "What if this fails like the nutrition business?"
- **Reframe:** "Each previous attempt taught me something crucial for this moment."
- **Challenge:** "Who am I to run a recovery home?"

- **Reframe:** "My experience makes me exactly the right person to understand what others need."

Visualization With Purpose

Before important meetings, challenging conversations, or potential trigger situations, I take time to mentally rehearse. But here's the key difference between effective visualization and just daydreaming: You have to visualize both the challenges and your response to them.

For example, before my first speaking engagement about recovery, I didn't just visualize success. I visualized:

- The moment of walking onto the stage with my past fully visible
- The weight of responsibility in sharing my story
- The potential skepticism in the room
- My centered response to each scenario

This kind of mental preparation isn't about eliminating anxiety; it's about channeling it into focused energy.

From Prison to Purpose: The Ultimate Reframe

One of the most powerful shifts in my thinking came when I stopped seeing prison as something that happened to me and started seeing it as something that happened for me. This wasn't about minimizing the experience or its consequences; it was about finding purpose in the pain.

When I first started working with others in recovery, I realized that my darkest experiences had given me a unique ability to connect with those still struggling. The very things that I thought would forever hold me back became my greatest assets in helping others move forward.

The Compound Effect of Mental Training

Just like physical training, mental resilience builds over time through consistent practice. Each time you:

- Face a trigger without retreating
- Share your story without shame
- Take responsibility without self-condemnation
- Embrace a challenge without guarantees

You're not just handling that specific situation better; you're rebuilding your entire relationship with adversity.

The Integration of Mind and Action

Here's something crucial I've learned: Mindset work isn't just about what happens in your head. It has to translate into action. When I started my business, positive thinking alone wouldn't secure locations, satisfy regulations, or build trust with families.

The real power of mental resilience shows up in how it changes your actions:

- Instead of avoiding difficult conversations, you initiate them.
- Instead of hiding your past, you leverage it for others' benefit.
- Instead of seeking comfort, you pursue growth.

Understanding the Biochemistry of Change

The mind-body connection isn't just a metaphor; it's a biological reality. When we engage in mental resilience practices, we're actually changing our biochemistry:

- **Stress reduction:** Lower cortisol levels
- **Emotional regulation:** Balanced serotonin and dopamine
- **Focus and clarity:** Increased BDNF (brain-derived neurotrophic factor)
- **Physical energy:** Improved mitochondrial function
- **Immune function:** Enhanced natural killer cell activity

This understanding helps explain why mental resilience practices have such profound effects on both our psychological and physical well-being.

Celebrating Progress While Staying Hungry

One of the trickiest balances in maintaining mental toughness is learning to celebrate progress without losing your edge. After each small win—landing a job, helping a resident, completing a challenging project—I take time to acknowledge the growth while staying focused on the next goal.

This isn't about perfectionism. It's about maintaining momentum while appreciating how far you've come. Every day at Elevate Recovery Homes, I see people battling their own internal dialogues, fighting for a new way of thinking about themselves and their possibilities. Their struggles and successes remind me that this work never really ends; it just evolves.

Looking Ahead: The Mind-Body Connection

As we move into the next chapter about the connection between physical and mental resilience, remember this: Your mind and body aren't separate systems. They're part of one integrated whole. The mental strength we've discussed here isn't just about thinking differently; it's about creating new patterns that affect every aspect of your being.

The practices we've explored—reframing, visualization, gratitude, and embracing challenges—create physical changes in your brain and body. They affect how you carry yourself, how you breathe, and how you move through the world.

Your mindset isn't just about what you think; it's about who you become. Every challenge becomes an opportunity. Every setback becomes a setup for a comeback. Every moment, no matter how difficult, contains the seed of something valuable.

Remember: The conversations you have with yourself are the most important conversations you'll ever have. Make them count because, in the end, resilience isn't just about bouncing back; it's about bouncing forward, using every experience, every challenge, and every setback as fuel for growth.

In the next chapter, we'll explore how to align your physical practices with this mental foundation, creating a complete system of resilience that serves you in every aspect of life. True resilience isn't just mental or physical; it's about integrating both into a powerful force for positive change in your life and the lives of others.

7

RESILIENCE THROUGH HEALTH-BODY AND MIND CONNECTION

L et me tell you about the moment I truly understood the connection between physical and mental resilience. I was 36 hours into the 4x4x48 Challenge—running four miles every four hours for 48 hours straight. My body was screaming for rest, running on just fragments of sleep. But something remarkable was happening in my mind.

From the start, I'd made an unshakeable decision: I would finish, no matter what. This wasn't a casual experiment or a "Let's see how it goes" situation. I'd already decided the outcome, and that mental commitment became the backbone that carried my body through what seemed impossible.

The Physical Foundations of Resilience

What I've learned through challenges like this is that physical resilience isn't just about being tough or pushing through pain. It's about building a foundation that supports your mental strength, and vice versa. They're not separate systems; they're one integrated whole.

The Science Behind Physical-Mental Integration

Recent neuroscience research has revealed fascinating connections between physical activity and mental resilience. When we exercise, our bodies release not just endorphins, but also proteins like BDNF (brain-derived neurotrophic factor) that literally help our brains grow stronger and more adaptable (Arida & Teixeira-Machado, 2021). This biological connection explains why physical training has such a profound impact on our mental state.

During intense physical challenges, our bodies also produce norepinephrine—a neurotransmitter that improves attention, perception, and emotional resilience. This explains why after a challenging workout, we often feel mentally sharper and emotionally more stable. Understanding these biological mechanisms helped me appreciate why the 4x4x48 Challenge wasn't just a physical test; it was rewiring my brain for greater resilience.

The impact of physical exercise on mental resilience goes beyond just these immediate neurochemical changes. Regular physical training creates lasting structural changes in the brain, particularly in regions associated with stress management, emotional regulation, and decision-making. The hippocampus—crucial for memory and learning—actually grows larger in response to consistent physical activity. Meanwhile, the amygdala—our brain's fear center—becomes better regulated, leading to improved emotional control during challenging situations.

The Decision That Precedes Action

During those early runs of the 4x4x48, my body felt strong, and my energy was high. But as the hours ticked by and night set in, exhaustion started to creep in. Running on two or three hours of sleep was brutal, and my body felt every step. But because I'd already locked in my decision to complete the challenge, there was no mental debate, no wavering.

This is crucial to understand: Physical resilience starts with mental commitment. I didn't waste energy asking myself if I could keep going. The answer was already decided. Each run became about staying steady, pacing myself, and keeping my form. The fatigue was real, but I let it pass through me without giving it any power.

The Psychology of Pre-Commitment

This pre-commitment strategy isn't just a mental trick; it's a powerful psychological tool backed by research. When we make firm decisions in advance, we activate different neural pathways than when we rely on in-the-moment willpower. This is why writing down our goals and making public commitments can be so effective. During the challenge, I shared my intention with friends and family, creating an additional layer of accountability that strengthened my resolve.

The power of pre-commitment lies in how it changes our relationship with challenge. Instead of facing each difficult moment as a new decision point, we've already charted our course. This reduces the cognitive load during challenging moments and preserves our mental energy for execution rather than deliberation. Research in behavioral psychology shows that this kind of advanced decision-making activates the prefrontal cortex, the part of our brain responsible for planning and complex decision-making while reducing activity in the limbic system, which drives our emotional responses to discomfort (Lin & Feng, 2024).

When I committed to the 4x4x48 Challenge, I didn't just say I would try—I made a binding contract with myself. I wrote down my commitment, shared it publicly, and most importantly, I spent time visualizing and accepting the inevitable difficulties I would face. This wasn't about being overconfident or ignoring the challenge ahead. Rather, it was about acknowledging the difficulty and choosing it anyway. This mental preparation created a psychological framework that would later prove invaluable during the darkest hours of the challenge.

Building the Foundation

Physical training builds more than just muscle and endurance. It creates a platform for mental toughness. With each challenging workout, each early morning training session, you're not just strengthening your body; you're strengthening your resolve. This foundation is built through a systematic approach that integrates physical conditioning with mental preparation.

Start With Commitment

The journey to physical resilience begins with establishing clear, nonnegotiable commitments. These aren't just casual promises to yourself; they're fundamental principles that guide your actions and decisions. The key is to make these commitments specific and measurable while aligning them with your deeper values and long-term goals.

Your commitment must extend beyond the surface level of wanting to "get in shape" or "be healthier." It needs to connect with your core values and life purpose. For instance, when I committed to building physical resilience, it wasn't just about achieving certain fitness metrics. It was about becoming someone who could be relied upon in crisis, someone who had the strength to support others when things got tough.

This level of commitment requires careful thought and preparation. Start by examining your motivations—what drives you to pursue physical resilience? What larger purpose will it serve in your life? Write these commitments down, but don't stop there. Create a detailed plan for how you'll honor them, including specific actions you'll take when faced with common obstacles.

Progressive Challenge

The path to physical and mental resilience requires a carefully calibrated approach to increasing difficulty. This isn't about randomly pushing your limits; it's about systematic progression that builds both capability and confidence. The key lies in understanding how to structure challenges that sit at the edge of your current abilities without crossing into counterproductive territory.

Each progression should serve multiple purposes. While you're building physical capacity, you're simultaneously developing mental fortitude. For example, when increasing running distance, you're not just strengthening your cardiovascular system and muscles—you're also teaching your mind to handle longer periods of sustained effort. This dual-purpose training creates a feedback loop where physical and mental growth reinforce each other.

Understanding the difference between productive discomfort and harmful pain becomes crucial in this progression. This discernment isn't just about injury prevention; it's about developing the wisdom to push boundaries effectively. Through experience, you learn to recognize the subtle signals your body sends when you're approaching real limits versus temporary discomfort. This knowledge becomes invaluable not just in training, but in all challenging life situations.

The progression itself should follow a wave pattern rather than a linear increase. Periods of intense challenge should be followed by periods of consolidation, where you practice and reinforce your new capabilities. This rhythm prevents burnout while ensuring that adaptations are properly integrated before moving to the next level.

Mindful Movement

Physical training reaches its full potential when combined with mindful awareness. This isn't about simply going through the motions; it's about developing a deep connection between body and mind during movement. Every session becomes an opportunity to practice presence and build body awareness.

Form and technique serve as anchors for this mindful practice. When you focus intensely on the quality of each movement, you naturally enter a state of presence. This attention to detail does more than prevent injury—it creates a feedback loop that enhances both physical performance and mental focus. The precision required for proper form demands full attention, naturally quieting the mental chatter that often disrupts our focus.

This mindful approach transforms routine physical training into a form of moving meditation. Whether you're lifting weights, running, or practicing yoga, each movement becomes an opportunity to develop presence and awareness. This practice has profound effects that extend far beyond the gym or training ground. The ability to maintain focused attention during physical challenges translates directly to other areas of life where mental clarity under pressure is essential.

The integration of mindfulness into movement also develops proprioception—your body's ability to sense its position and movement in space. This enhanced body awareness becomes a valuable tool for managing stress and maintaining composure in challenging situations. When you can feel tension building in your body, you can address it before it affects your performance or decision-making.

The Neuroscience of Physical Training

The transformation that occurs in our brains during physical training is nothing short of remarkable. Each training session initiates a cascade of neurological adaptations that enhance both physical and mental capabilities. Understanding these changes helps us appreciate why physical training is so powerful for developing overall resilience.

Strengthening Neural Pathways

The brain's adaptability, known as neuroplasticity, is enhanced through physical training in ways that transform our capabilities. When we engage in challenging physical activity, we're not just building muscle; we're creating and strengthening neural connections that improve overall brain function.

The communication between different brain regions becomes more efficient through regular training. This enhanced neural connectivity improves everything from motor control to emotional regulation. The corpus callosum—the bridge between our brain's hemispheres—actually becomes denser with regular physical activity, leading to better coordination between logical and intuitive thinking.

Our stress response mechanisms undergo significant refinement through training. Regular exposure to physical challenges helps optimize the hypothalamic-pituitary-adrenal (HPA) axis, our body's primary stress response system. This optimization leads to more appropriate responses to stressors—neither under-reacting nor overreacting to challenges.

Emotional regulation improves as the connection between our prefrontal cortex and limbic system strengthens. This enhanced communication allows us to better manage emotional responses during challenging situations. The result is greater emotional stability and resilience, even in high-pressure situations.

The development of cognitive flexibility through physical training is particularly fascinating. Complex movement patterns and varied training protocols challenge our brains to adapt quickly to changing demands. This adaptability transfers to other areas of life, improving our ability to handle unexpected situations and find creative solutions to problems.

Hormonal Optimization

Physical training creates a sophisticated orchestration of hormonal responses that enhance both our physical and mental capabilities. This hormonal optimization isn't just about temporary changes; it fundamentally reshapes our body's chemical environment to support greater resilience.

The regulation of cortisol, often called the stress hormone, becomes more refined through regular training. While untrained individuals might experience dramatic cortisol spikes in response to stress, those who train regularly develop a more nuanced cortisol response. Their bodies learn to produce appropriate amounts of cortisol when needed for focus and energy while maintaining lower baseline levels that support recovery and mental clarity.

Insulin sensitivity improves markedly with consistent physical training. This enhancement goes far beyond blood sugar control—it affects our energy levels, mood stability, and cognitive function throughout the day. Better insulin sensitivity means more stable energy levels, which translates to more consistent mental performance and emotional stability.

Growth hormone production, particularly during sleep and recovery periods, increases with regular training. This hormone isn't just about physical repair and renewal; it plays a crucial role in brain health and cognitive function. The pulsatile release of growth hormone helps optimize both physical recovery and mental restoration, supporting everything from memory consolidation to emotional processing.

Testosterone levels, important for both men and women, find their optimal balance through regular training. This hormonal optimization supports not just physical strength and recovery, but also confidence, motivation, and mental resilience. The key is finding the right training intensity and volume to promote healthy testosterone levels without triggering excessive stress responses.

Cellular Adaptation

At the cellular level, physical training triggers remarkable adaptations that enhance our resilience from the ground up. These changes occur not just in our muscles, but throughout our entire body, including our brain and nervous system.

The increase in mitochondrial density represents one of the most significant cellular adaptations to training. These cellular powerhouses become more numerous and efficient, providing better energy production not just for physical activity, but for all bodily functions, including cognitive processes. This enhanced cellular energy capacity means better performance under stress and faster recovery from all types of challenges.

Protein synthesis becomes more efficient with regular training, improving our body's ability to repair and strengthen tissues. This enhanced protein synthesis isn't limited to muscles; it extends to neural tissue, supporting better brain function and faster recovery from mental exertion. The body becomes more adept at producing the proteins needed for both structural repair and signaling molecules that support cognitive function.

Our cellular repair mechanisms undergo significant enhancement through regular training. The body becomes more efficient at identifying and fixing cellular damage, removing waste products, and optimizing cellular function. This improved repair capacity extends to neural tissue, supporting better brain health and cognitive resilience.

The development of stress proteins, particularly heat shock proteins and other cellular protective mechanisms, provides another layer of resilience. These molecular chaperones help protect cellular components from damage during various types of stress, whether physical or psychological. This enhanced cellular protection means better tolerance for all types of stressors.

The Power of Nutrition in Resilience

Nutrition serves as the fundamental building block of both physical and mental resilience. Through years of research and personal experimentation, I've discovered that what we eat doesn't just fuel our bodies; it shapes our capacity for handling stress, maintaining focus, and recovering from challenges of all kinds.

Fueling for Mental Clarity

The relationship between nutrition and mental performance goes far deeper than simple energy provision. Every meal we consume triggers a complex cascade of biochemical reactions that influence our cognitive function, emotional stability, and stress resilience.

During those long hours on big projects, I discovered that the right nutritional strategy could mean the difference between mental fog and crystal clarity. This wasn't just about avoiding hunger; it was about providing my brain with the optimal fuel mixture for sustained high performance. Through careful attention to my diet,

I learned to maintain steady energy levels and sharp focus throughout demanding days.

The transformation in my mental performance was dramatic. Gone were the mid-afternoon energy crashes that used to plague my workdays. Instead, I maintained consistent mental clarity and emotional stability, even under significant pressure. This wasn't achieved through stimulants or quick fixes but through a deep understanding of how different foods affect brain function and mental performance.

The Biochemistry of Resilience

Understanding the complex biochemistry of nutrition has revolutionized how I approach both physical and mental challenges. Our bodies are sophisticated chemical factories, and every nutrient we consume plays a vital role in our capacity for resilience. This isn't just about calories or macronutrients; it's about providing our bodies with the precise materials needed to build and maintain resilience at a cellular level.

Essential Fatty Acids

The role of essential fatty acids in building resilience extends far beyond basic nutrition. Omega-3 fatty acids, particularly DHA and EPA, serve as fundamental building blocks for brain tissue and neurotransmitter production. These fatty acids become incorporated into cell membranes throughout the nervous system, improving neural communication and supporting cognitive function under stress.

Medium-chain triglycerides provide a unique form of energy that can be rapidly utilized by both body and brain. Unlike long-chain fatty acids, MCTs can cross the blood-brain barrier efficiently, providing an alternative energy source for neural tissue. This becomes particularly important during extended periods of stress or physical exertion when glucose metabolism might be compromised.

Phospholipids serve as crucial components of cell membranes throughout the body, particularly in neural tissue. Their proper balance ensures optimal membrane fluidity and function, which is essential for everything from neurotransmitter release to hormone receptor sensitivity. Regular consumption of phospholipid-rich foods supports both the structural integrity and functional capacity of neural networks.

Beyond their structural roles, essential fatty acids serve as precursors for hormone production throughout the body. The balance of different fatty acids in our diet influences our hormonal milieu, affecting everything from inflammation responses to stress hormone production. This hormonal optimization becomes crucial for maintaining resilience under challenging conditions.

Micronutrient Support

The role of micronutrients in resilience extends far beyond preventing deficiency diseases. These essential vitamins and minerals serve as cofactors in countless biochemical reactions that support both physical and mental performance.

B vitamins function as crucial cofactors in energy metabolism, neurotransmitter production, and DNA repair. Their proper balance is essential for maintaining mental energy and emotional stability. Each member of the B-vitamin family plays specific roles in neural function and stress response mechanisms. For example, B6 is crucial for serotonin production, while B12 supports myelin maintenance and nerve function.

Magnesium's role in nervous system function can't be overstated. This mineral serves as a natural calming agent, regulating neurotransmitter release and supporting healthy stress responses.

Adequate magnesium levels help maintain stable mood and energy levels while supporting recovery from both physical and mental exertion. In times of stress, magnesium requirements increase significantly, making regular replenishment crucial for resilience.

Zinc plays multiple roles in supporting resilience, from immune system function to neurotransmitter regulation. This mineral is particularly important during periods of high stress, as it supports both tissue repair and proper hormone production. Zinc deficiency can compromise both physical recovery and mental clarity, making its adequate intake essential for maintaining resilience.

Vitamin D's influence extends far beyond bone health, affecting everything from immune function to mood regulation. This hormone-like vitamin modulates gene expression throughout the body, influencing our capacity for both physical and mental resilience. Adequate vitamin D levels support healthy stress responses, immune function, and cognitive performance.

Antioxidant Protection

The role of antioxidants in building resilience goes beyond simple protection against oxidative stress. These compounds serve as signaling molecules that trigger adaptive responses throughout the body, enhancing our capacity to handle various types of stress.

Polyphenols, found abundantly in colorful fruits and vegetables, provide more than just cellular protection. These compounds influence gene expression and cellular signaling pathways, promoting adaptations that enhance overall resilience. Different classes of polyphenols work synergistically to support various aspects of health, from cardiovascular function to cognitive performance.

Flavonoids serve as powerful anti-inflammatory compounds that help modulate our response to various stressors. These compounds can cross the blood-brain barrier, providing direct support for neural tissue while reducing inflammation throughout the body. Regular consumption of flavonoid-rich foods helps maintain optimal brain function and supports recovery from both physical and mental challenges.

Carotenoids provide essential protection for neural tissue while supporting visual processing and cognitive function. These fat-soluble compounds accumulate in neural tissue, where they help protect against oxidative damage while supporting healthy cell signaling. Their presence in the brain and retina becomes particularly important during periods of high cognitive demand or visual stress.

Vitamin C plays multiple roles in supporting resilience, from collagen synthesis to neurotransmitter production. This versatile nutrient supports both immune function and stress response mechanisms while protecting tissues from oxidative damage. Its water-soluble nature necessitates regular replenishment, particularly during periods of high stress or physical exertion.

Building a Resilience-Based Nutrition Plan

The development of a nutrition plan that supports resilience requires more than just following general healthy eating guidelines. It demands a sophisticated understanding of how different foods and nutrients interact with our body's systems, particularly under stress.

Quality Matters

The quality of our nutritional choices has far-reaching implications for resilience that extend well beyond immediate energy provision. When selecting foods to support brain function, we must consider not just their macronutrient content, but their full spectrum of bioactive compounds. For example, wild-caught fish provide not just protein, but also essential fatty acids and minerals in forms that are highly bioavailable and supportive of cognitive function.

Understanding how different foods affect mood and energy requires careful attention to personal response patterns. Through systematic observation, we can identify which combinations of foods provide stable energy and clear thinking, versus those that lead to energy crashes or mental fog. This isn't just about avoiding processed foods or sugar—it's about optimizing our nutritional choices for peak mental and physical performance.

The focus on consistent, sustainable nutrition becomes particularly crucial during periods of high stress. Rather than reaching for quick fixes or stimulants, developing a foundation of nutrient-dense foods ensures that our bodies have the resources needed to maintain resilience. This might mean preparing meals in advance, keeping healthy snacks readily available, and developing strategies for maintaining good nutrition even when time is limited.

Timing Is Critical

The timing of our nutritional intake plays a crucial role in maintaining resilience throughout the day. Maintaining steady energy levels requires more than just regular meals; it demands strategic timing of different nutrients to support our body's natural rhythms and energy demands.

Eating to support activity and recovery needs becomes particularly important when training for resilience. Pre-workout nutrition should provide readily available energy while supporting focus and performance. Post-workout nutrition needs to emphasize repair and recovery, with adequate protein and carbohydrates to replenish depleted resources and support adaptation.

The practice of staying ahead of hunger serves multiple purposes in building resilience. When we wait until we're extremely hungry to eat, we're more likely to make poor food choices and overeat. Moreover, significant hunger can impair decision-making and emotional regulation—two key aspects of resilience. Planning meals and snacks to prevent extreme hunger helps maintain both physical and mental performance.

Mindful Eating

The practice of mindful eating extends beyond simply paying attention to our food; it becomes a tool for understanding how different foods affect our mental state and performance. By carefully observing the effects of different foods on our energy, mood, and cognitive function, we can optimize our nutrition for resilience.

Meal preparation becomes a form of self-care when approached mindfully. The process of planning, preparing, and consuming nutritious meals creates a positive feedback loop that reinforces healthy choices and builds confidence in our ability to maintain resilience-supporting habits. This isn't just about the nutritional content of the food; it's about developing a healthy relationship with eating that supports overall well-being.

Creating sustainable habits requires understanding the difference between rigid diets and flexible, sustainable nutritional approaches. Instead of following strict rules that may be difficult to maintain under stress, we develop principles and guidelines that can adapt to different situations while still supporting our resilience goals. This might mean having several go-to meals that we know support our performance or developing strategies for maintaining good nutrition during travel or high-stress periods.

The Recovery Revolution

The transformation in our understanding of recovery has fundamentally changed how we approach resilience training. What was once seen as merely rest has been revealed as an active process of adaptation and enhancement that's crucial for building both physical and mental resilience.

The Art of Strategic Rest

The integration of active recovery routines marks a sophisticated evolution in our approach to building resilience. Traditional static rest has been replaced by a more nuanced understanding of how different recovery activities can enhance adaptation and prevent burnout.

Flexibility work has emerged as a crucial component of recovery, but its benefits extend beyond simple muscle lengthening. Through focused stretching sessions, we can improve tissue quality while also creating opportunities for mental relaxation and stress release. Dynamic flexibility work helps maintain range of motion while promoting blood flow and tissue repair.

Self-myofascial release through foam rolling has revolutionized our approach to tissue maintenance and recovery. This practice goes beyond simple muscle recovery—it helps regulate the autonomic nervous system, promoting parasympathetic activation and stress reduction. The careful attention required for effective foam rolling also creates opportunities for mindfulness and body awareness.

The integration of yoga into recovery practices provides benefits that extend far beyond physical flexibility. Through mindful movement and breath work, yoga helps bridge the gap between physical and mental recovery. The practice develops body awareness, promotes parasympathetic activation, and enhances the mind-body connection that's crucial for resilience.

The implementation of planned rest days represents a mature understanding of the role of recovery in building resilience. Rather than viewing rest days as lost training opportunities, we recognize them as essential components of adaptation and growth. These days become opportunities for mental recovery, skill consolidation, and preparation for future challenges.

The Science of Strategic Recovery

Modern research has revolutionized our understanding of recovery processes, revealing sophisticated mechanisms that support both physical and mental resilience. This knowledge allows us to optimize recovery protocols for maximum benefit.

Sleep Architecture

Understanding the complexity of sleep cycles has transformed how we approach recovery. Each stage of sleep serves specific restoration functions, from physical repair during deep sleep to memory consolidation and emotional processing during REM sleep. Optimizing sleep architecture involves more than just getting enough hours; it requires attention to sleep timing, environment, and pre-sleep routines.

The deep sleep phases prove particularly crucial for physical restoration. During these periods, growth hormone release peaks, promoting tissue repair and adaptation. Understanding this timing helps us structure training and recovery schedules to maximize adaptation.

REM sleep plays a vital role in emotional resilience and cognitive processing. During REM periods, the brain processes emotional experiences and consolidates learning from the previous day. Ensuring adequate REM sleep becomes particularly important during periods of intense training or high stress.

Circadian rhythm alignment emerges as a fundamental aspect of recovery optimization. By synchronizing our activities with our natural biological rhythms, we can enhance both the quality and efficiency of our recovery processes.

Looking Ahead: Preparing for Crisis

As we conclude this exploration of physical and mental resilience, it's crucial to understand how these foundations prepare us for life's inevitable challenges. The physical capabilities, mental strength, and recovery practices we develop become invaluable resources during times of crisis.

The repository of strength we build through consistent training serves as more than just physical capacity; it becomes a wellspring of confidence and capability that we can draw upon when faced with any challenge. Every aspect of our training, from the physical workouts to the nutritional habits and recovery practices, contributes to our overall resilience.

Remember that true resilience isn't about being invulnerable; it's about having the capacity to face challenges, adapt to circumstances, and recover effectively. The integration of physical training, proper nutrition, and strategic recovery creates a comprehensive framework for developing this capacity.

As you move forward in your own resilience journey, maintain perspective on the larger purpose of this work. While the immediate benefits of improved physical fitness and mental clarity are valuable, the true power lies in the enhanced capacity to handle life's challenges with grace and effectiveness.

Continue to approach your training with curiosity and commitment, knowing that each session, each meal, and each recovery period contributes to your overall resilience. Stay open to new insights and adaptations, but remain grounded in the fundamental principles we've explored:

- Physical training builds more than just strength; it develops capacity for all types of challenges.
- Nutrition provides the foundation for both physical and mental performance.
- Recovery isn't just rest; it's an active process of adaptation and growth.
- Mental and physical resilience are inseparable aspects of overall capability.

The future will undoubtedly bring new challenges and opportunities. By maintaining and building upon these foundations of resilience, you'll be prepared to face whatever comes with confidence and capability.

Your journey in building resilience is ongoing, and each day brings new opportunities for growth and development. Embrace these opportunities, knowing that you're not just building physical strength or mental toughness, but developing an integrated capacity for resilience that will serve you in all aspects of life.

The science of resilience continues to evolve, revealing new insights into how we can optimize our training, nutrition, and recovery. Stay informed about these developments, but remember that the fundamental principles we've discussed remain constant. The integration of physical and mental training, supported by proper nutrition and recovery, creates a foundation for resilience that can weather any storm.

As you continue on your path, remember that resilience is not a destination but a journey. Each challenge becomes an opportunity to apply and refine these principles, and each setback becomes a chance to demonstrate and strengthen your resilience. The future belongs to those who prepare for it, and through the dedicated application of these principles, you're building the capacity to face that future with confidence and capability.

This isn't just about being fit or eating well; it's about building an unshakeable foundation for whatever life throws your way. When your body and mind work as one, there's no limit to what you can overcome. Trust in your training, maintain your practices, and keep building your resilience, one day at a time.

8

CRISIS MODE-RESILIENCE IN TIMES
OF EXTREME ADVERSITY

That first night at Bite Club, the kitchen felt alive with possibility. My business partner and I had spent months planning every detail of our athlete-focused meal prep service. The air was thick with the aroma of herbs and spices as we perfected recipes, calculated macros, and dreamed about the impact we'd make. We weren't just creating meals; we were building something we believed would transform how athletes approached nutrition.

Those early days were filled with endless possibilities. We visited local suppliers, negotiating the best prices for the highest quality ingredients. Late nights were spent tweaking recipes, ensuring each meal delivered precise nutrition without sacrificing taste. Every detail mattered—from the way we packaged the food to maintain freshness, to mapping delivery routes for maximum efficiency. We approached each aspect with the same dedication athletes bring to their training.

But sometimes crisis creeps in quietly, hiding in spreadsheets and profit margins. After each production run, we'd analyze the numbers, looking for ways to reduce costs without compromising quality. It was like trying to solve an impossible equation—our commitment to excellence constantly battling against the harsh realities of food service economics. Each meal we sold barely covered costs, but we kept pushing, believing we could eventually make it work.

Then COVID-19 hit, and everything changed overnight.

The world transformed in ways we couldn't have imagined. Supply chains fractured, causing our costs to soar. Gyms closed, decimating our target market. Safety regulations added new burdens to our already strained operations. Standing in that same kitchen that had once felt so full of promise, I now faced the hardest decision of my entrepreneurial journey.

The toughest moment wasn't deciding to close; it was standing there surrounded by ingredients we could no longer afford to use, watching months of work and planning slip away. Not because we hadn't tried hard enough or planned well enough, but because sometimes the world changes in ways you can't control.

This moment taught me something crucial about crisis: Your initial response shapes everything that follows. In those first moments, when everything you've built seems to be crumbling, your instinct is to react immediately, to try to fix everything at once. But true resilience requires something different—the ability to pause, assess, and respond with clarity rather than fear.

Running a business during a crisis isn't just about managing oper-ations; it's about leading people through uncertainty. I remember one particularly challenging week when everything seemed to be falling apart simultaneously. We'd lost a major client, one of my key team members was struggling with personal issues and missing deadlines, and the pressure to hit our targets was mount-ing. I could feel the frustration building inside me like a pressure cooker, every instinct screaming to let that stress spill over onto my team.

The Weight of Leadership

In that moment of mounting pressure on my team, I learned something fundamental about crisis management: Your response as a leader ripples through everyone around you. I stepped outside the office, away from the noise and tension, to reset. This wasn't about suppressing emotions; it was about processing them prop-erly so I could lead effectively.

Standing there, taking deep breaths in the quiet, I reminded myself that I wasn't just carrying my own stress. Every person on that team trusted me with their livelihood, their professional growth, and their daily peace of mind. If I let my frustration dictate my response, I'd multiply the pressure everyone was already feeling.

When I walked back into the office, I approached our challenges differently. Instead of letting the stress of our lost client and missed deadlines drive the conversation, I focused on creating space for solutions. We spent the afternoon brainstorming new approaches, each team member contributing ideas from their perspective. By day's end, the tension had begun to ease, replaced by a collective sense of purpose.

The Art of Letting Go

The decision to close Bite Club wasn't a single moment but a series of small surrenders. Each day brought new evidence that our carefully constructed plans were becoming unsustainable.

We'd built something with such precision and care—every recipe perfected, every process streamlined, every detail considered. Watching it slip away taught me that sometimes resilience isn't about holding on tighter; it's about knowing when to let go.

This wasn't just about closing a business. It was about understanding that failure isn't always about a lack of effort or vision. Sometimes the world simply changes in ways you can't control, and your resilience is measured not by your ability to prevent the inevitable, but by how you choose to move forward from it.

Finding Purpose in Crisis

Looking back now, I can see how each setback was preparing me for something larger. The meticulous attention to detail we developed at Bite Club, the understanding of sustainable business practices, the lessons in leading teams through difficult times—none of that learning was wasted. Every spreadsheet analysis, every team management challenge, every difficult decision was building the skills I'd need to help others in recovery.

The transition from failed ventures to building successful behavioral health businesses wasn't immediate or easy. After each setback, I had to resist both the urge to give up entirely and the temptation to rush into the next venture without processing the lessons of the last. Instead, I learned to sit with the discomfort of failure, to extract every possible lesson from the experience, and to understand how each challenge was shaping me for what would come next.

The Phoenix Principle: Rising From Crisis

Each failure became a building block for what would come next. After Bite Club, I launched another business venture, then another. Each one taught me something crucial about resilience, adaptation, and the delicate balance between holding onto vision and knowing when to pivot.

What I didn't realize during those difficult moments was how every challenge was actually preparing me for my true calling. The same attention to detail that went into perfecting meal prep recipes would later help me create structured recovery programs. The skills I developed in managing team emotions during a crisis became invaluable in supporting people through their recovery journey. Even the hard lessons about sustainable business models shaped how I would eventually build my healthcare businesses.

The Deeper Layers of Crisis Management

Leading a team through a crisis reveals layers of resilience you never knew you had. I remember sitting in meetings, watching my team grapple with uncertainty, knowing that my response to each challenge would either strengthen or weaken their own resilience. It wasn't just about maintaining composure; it was about demonstrating that it's possible to face reality honestly while maintaining hope.

During particularly tough periods, I developed a practice of processing my own reactions before engaging with the team. Sometimes this meant taking early morning walks to clear my head, or staying late to work through concerns after everyone had left. The goal wasn't to hide the challenges but to approach them with the kind of clarity that inspires confidence rather than anxiety.

The Recovery Blueprint

When you're in the middle of a crisis, it's impossible to see the full picture. Standing in that empty Bite Club kitchen, watching our dream dissolve, I couldn't have imagined how those painful lessons would eventually serve a greater purpose. But that's the nature of resilience; it's built in layers, often invisible until you need them most.

The recovery process taught me that bouncing back isn't about returning to where you were; it's about building something better based on what you've learned. Each failed venture added to my understanding of what creates sustainable success:

From the athlete meal prep service, I learned the importance of viable business models alongside passionate vision. From managing teams through difficult transitions, I gained insight into how people process change and challenges. From having to close businesses I'd poured my heart into, I learned how to help others face their own losses and transitions with grace.

Building my behavioral health businesses became possible not despite these failures, but because of them. Every setback had taught me something essential about human nature, about resilience, about the delicate balance between supporting people and empowering them to support themselves.

The Transformation Through Crisis

Now, working with members in one of our programs, I see how crisis reveals not just our vulnerabilities but our deepest strengths. When someone walks through our doors, they're often facing their own version of standing in that empty kitchen, watching dreams crumble. But I can tell them with absolute certainty that crisis isn't the end of their story; it's often the beginning of a better one.

The skills I developed managing businesses through difficult times translate directly into helping others navigate their recovery journey. I understand now that resilience isn't about being unbreakable; it's about learning how to put yourself back together stronger than before. Every spreadsheet I analyzed, every team I led through uncertainty, and every difficult decision I had to make was preparing me to help others find their way through their own challenges.

The Reality of Rebuilding

Recovery after a crisis isn't a straight line. When we had to shut down Bite Club, I went through phases of doubt, questioning every decision that led to that moment. The same happened with each subsequent venture that didn't succeed. But each time, the recovery process became more structured and more intentional. I learned to treat setbacks not as endpoints but as data points— valuable information about what works, what doesn't, and what needs to change.

This lesson proves invaluable now in working with people in recovery. I can show them through my own experience that failure isn't fatal; it's informative. The same principles that helped me rebuild after business setbacks apply to rebuilding life after addiction: honest assessment, strategic planning, consistent action, and perhaps most importantly, the willingness to learn and adapt.

The Long View of Resilience

Looking back at all these experiences—from the excitement of launching Bite Club to the pain of closing it, from subsequent ventures to building Elevate Recovery Homes, True North Recovery Services, and All The Way Well, I see how each crisis shaped not just my path but my ability to help others find theirs. The very challenges that could have broken me instead became the foundation for something meaningful.

When I work with someone struggling in their recovery journey, I can share authentically about the power of persistence, not from theory but from lived experience. I understand the fear of starting over, the weight of past failures, and the uncertainty of new beginnings. But I also know firsthand the incredible strength that can emerge from these challenges.

Moving Forward: The Continuous Journey

A crisis isn't something you face once and then move past. It's a continuous process of growth, adaptation, and renewal. Each challenge—whether in business, recovery, or life—presents an opportunity to build greater resilience. The key isn't to avoid crisis; it's to develop the tools, mindset, and support systems that allow you to navigate it effectively.

As we move into discussing adaptation to life's unpredictable changes, remember this: Your response to crisis doesn't just define your present moment; it shapes your future capacity for resilience. Every challenge you face either breaks you or builds you, and the difference lies in how you process and use the experience.

The journey of resilience is never really complete. Each crisis brings new lessons, new growth opportunities, and new chances to demonstrate the strength you've built. And perhaps most importantly, each challenge you overcome becomes a beacon of hope for others facing their own struggles.

This is the ultimate purpose of resilience—not just to survive our own challenges, but to light the way for others to find their path through darkness. In the next chapter, we'll explore how to adapt to life's constant changes, using these crisis management skills to create sustainable success in an ever-changing world.

Remember: Crisis doesn't define you; it reveals you. And often, what it reveals is far stronger than you ever imagined possible.

9

EMBRACING CHANGE

S tanding in front of the municipal board, making our case for our first Elevate Home, I felt the weight of resistance pushing against everything we were trying to build. Each objection, each "concern" from the neighborhood, and each regulatory hurdle felt like another wall being erected between us and our mission. The easy response would have been to push back harder, to let frustration fuel a confrontational approach. But in that moment, I understood something crucial about change and resilience: Sometimes the path forward isn't about pushing harder; it's about adapting your approach while maintaining your commitment.

This lesson didn't come easily. Like many of life's most important teachings, it came through experience, through failure, through the hard work of rebuilding after everything familiar had been stripped away. From the roar of college football stadiums to the silence of a prison cell, from the highs of athletic achievement to the lows of addiction, my journey has been one of constant adaptation. Each transition taught me that resilience isn't about being unshakeable; it's about learning to bend without breaking.

Embracing Change: The Foundation of Resilience

Let me tell you about resistance to change. When I first entered recovery, every fiber of my being fought against the new reality I faced. I'd built my identity around being an athlete, around being "strong." The idea of admitting vulnerability, of accepting help, of completely reconstructing who I was—it felt like dying. And in a way, it was. The old version of me, the one who thought strength meant never showing weakness, had to die for something new to emerge.

This resistance to change runs deeper than mere stubbornness. Our neurological wiring predisposes us to seek stability, to grasp desperately at the familiar even when it's destroying us. The brain's threat response system activates when faced with significant change, triggering the same fight-or-flight mechanisms that protected our ancestors from physical dangers. But in today's world, this biological resistance to change often works against us, keeping us trapped in patterns that no longer serve our growth.

Through my recovery journey, I discovered that the very things I resisted most were often the catalysts for my most significant growth. Each time I surrendered to change instead of fighting it, I found new strengths I never knew I possessed. The process was never easy, but it became easier once I understood that resistance only prolonged the inevitable transformation.

The Paradox of Stability Through Change

What I've come to understand about change is deeply paradoxical: The more we embrace change, the more stable we become. This isn't about becoming chaotic or abandoning all structure; it's about developing what I call "dynamic stability," the ability to maintain your center while everything around you shifts.

Think about a skilled surfer riding a wave. They're not fighting against the water's movement; they're working with it, adjusting constantly while maintaining their balance. This is the kind of stability we need to cultivate—not the rigid stability of a building, but the dynamic stability of a living system that can adapt and flow with changing circumstances.

During my early days of recovery, I had to relearn everything I thought I knew about stability. My old approach of trying to control every aspect of my environment had failed spectacularly. The new path required learning to find stability within myself, regardless of external circumstances. This meant developing internal anchors that could weather any storm.

The Practice of Internal Anchoring

The development of internal stability begins with establishing consistent practices that ground you during times of change. These aren't just habits or routines; they're intentional practices that build your capacity for resilience. Through my work in the behavioral health space, I've seen how these internal anchors become crucial lifelines during times of transition.

Morning practices became particularly vital in my journey. Each day begins with a period of intentional grounding—not just going through the motions, but actively creating a foundation for whatever challenges might arise. This includes physical movement that connects me with my body, quiet reflection that centers my mind, and purposeful planning that directs my energy.

The Psychology of Adaptive Resilience

What I discovered through the process of establishing my businesses was that resilience isn't a static trait; it's a dynamic capacity that grows through conscious development. The psychology behind this growth reveals fascinating insights about how we can cultivate adaptability while maintaining our core purpose.

From Resistance to Flow

The transformation from resistance to adaptability doesn't happen overnight. It's a gradual process of rewiring our default responses to change. During our struggles with the municipal board, I witnessed this transformation firsthand. Each objection initially triggered my defensive mechanisms—the same ones that had once fueled my addiction. But through conscious practice, I learned to transform that defensive energy into creative problem-solving.

Consider how water responds to obstacles. It doesn't try to overpower them; it finds new pathways around them. This natural adaptability became our model at Elevate. When faced with neighborhood resistance, instead of fighting back, we began asking different questions: How could we address their legitimate concerns while staying true to our mission? What opportunities for community building were hidden within these challenges?

The Architecture of Adaptive Thinking

Developing adaptive thinking requires rebuilding our mental frameworks from the ground up. The rigid thought patterns that once seemed protective often become our greatest limitations. Through my work with residents at Elevate, I've observed how this reconstruction process unfolds in real time.

The first step involves recognizing our automatic responses to change. These deeply ingrained patterns often operate below our conscious awareness, driving reactions that don't serve our growth. By bringing these patterns into consciousness, we can begin to modify them. This isn't about suppressing our natural responses; it's about expanding our range of possible responses.

Next comes the development of what I call "strategic flexibility." This means maintaining strong principles while remaining flexible about methods. At Elevate and True North Recovery Services, our core mission is to support recovery never wavers, but our approaches to achieving that mission constantly evolve based on community needs, regulatory requirements, and the unique challenges of each resident.

Building Bridges Through Change

The process of establishing these recovery businesses taught me that successful adaptation often requires building bridges— between where we are and where we need to be, between different perspectives, and between seemingly opposing needs. This bridge-building becomes particularly crucial during times of significant change.

The Art of Stakeholder Integration

Working with the municipal board and neighborhood residents revealed the importance of integrating multiple perspectives into our adaptation process. Rather than seeing different stakeholders as obstacles, we learned to view them as essential partners in creating sustainable solutions.

This integration process begins with deep listening. Not the kind of listening that waits for a chance to respond, but the kind that seeks genuine understanding. When neighborhood residents expressed concerns about safety, we didn't dismiss them as NIMBYism. Instead, we saw an opportunity to demonstrate how recovery homes actually enhance community safety through structured support and accountability.

Through this process, we developed what I call "collaborative resilience"—the ability to build stronger solutions by incorporating diverse perspectives. This approach transformed potential adversaries into allies, creating a more robust and sustainable model for our business.

Maintaining Mission Through Adaptation

One of the most challenging aspects of change is maintaining your core purpose while adapting your methods. At Elevate, this meant holding firm to our commitment to recovery while remaining flexible about how we achieved it. This balance requires constant attention and regular reassessment.

The key lies in distinguishing between principles and practices. Principles are the foundational truths that guide your mission—they rarely change. Practices are the specific methods you use to apply those principles—these should remain flexible and responsive to circumstances.

For example, our core principle of providing safe, supportive environments for recovery never changes. But how we create those environments—the specific programs, policies, and procedures—continuously evolves based on what we learn works best for our residents and communities.

The Practice of Conscious Adaptation

Through years of working with individuals in recovery, I've learned that conscious adaptation is both an art and a science. It requires developing specific skills and practices that enable us to navigate change effectively while maintaining our core stability. This understanding didn't come easily—it emerged through countless hours of working with residents, facing organizational challenges, and personally navigating the complex landscape of recovery and business development.

The Art of Adaptation

The artistic element of conscious adaptation lies in its creative and intuitive aspects. Like a skilled artist who knows exactly how much pressure to apply to their brush, conscious adaptation requires a refined sense of when to push forward and when to yield. This intuitive understanding develops through experience and careful attention to both subtle and obvious signals.

I remember working with a resident who was struggling with our structured program schedule. The "scientific" approach would have been to simply enforce the rules rigidly. Instead, by applying the art of conscious adaptation, we noticed that his resistance peaked during certain types of group activities. Through careful observation and dialogue, we discovered he had undiagnosed social anxiety. Rather than forcing compliance, we worked with him to gradually build his comfort in group settings while temporarily modifying some requirements. This artistic approach to adaptation allowed him to stay in recovery while building crucial skills at a pace he could manage.

The Science of Adaptation

The scientific aspect of conscious adaptation involves understanding the measurable, repeatable elements of successful change. This includes recognizing pattern development, understanding behavioral triggers, and implementing evidence-based practices that support sustainable transformation.

At Elevate, True North, and All The Way Well, we've documented and analyzed hundreds of cases of successful and unsuccessful adaptations to recovery. This data has revealed clear patterns in how people navigate change effectively.

Pattern Recognition

We've identified specific stages that most people go through when adapting to significant life changes:

1. **Initial resistance phase:** Characterized by skepticism and defensive behaviors
2. **Contemplation stage:** Where individuals begin considering the potential benefits of change
3. **Experimental adaptation:** Small steps toward new behaviors and thinking patterns
4. **Integration period:** When new patterns begin feeling natural and sustainable
5. **Mastery phase:** Where adapted behaviors become automatic and can be taught to others

Neurological Understanding

The science of adaptation also involves understanding how our brains process and integrate change. Through partnerships with neuroscience researchers, we've learned how various practices can support the brain's natural adaptation processes:

- Regular routines create neural pathways that support new behaviors.
- Gradual exposure to change reduces stress responses and promotes learning.
- Social support activates reward centers that reinforce positive adaptations.
- Mindfulness practices strengthen the brain's ability to regulate emotions during change.

The Integration of Art and Science

The most effective approach to conscious adaptation comes from integrating both artistic and scientific elements. This integration manifests in several key ways:

1. Structured Flexibility

We develop frameworks that are scientifically sound yet flexible enough to accommodate individual differences. For example, our recovery program has clear, research-based structures, but we build in flexibility points where individual needs can be addressed without compromising the program's integrity.

1. Data-Informed Intuition

We train our staff to use both empirical evidence and intuitive understanding when working with residents. This means knowing the research and best practices while remaining attuned to the unique needs and circumstances of each individual.

1. Adaptive Assessment

Our evaluation processes combine quantitative metrics with qualitative observations. We track measurable outcomes while remaining attentive to the subtle signs of progress that numbers can't capture.

1. Progressive Refinement

Like any practice that combines art and science, conscious adaptation improves through consistent application and reflection. Each experience provides new insights that can be integrated into our understanding and approach.

The practice of conscious adaptation isn't just about managing change; it's about thriving through it. By developing this capacity, we build resilience that serves us not just in recovery or business, but in every aspect of life. It becomes a fundamental skill that allows us to maintain stability while continuing to grow and evolve.

The Implementation Framework

The practice of conscious adaptation requires a robust implementation framework that bridges theory and practice. Through our work in this field, we've developed a comprehensive approach that makes these concepts actionable in daily life.

1. Situational Awareness Training

One of the most crucial elements of conscious adaptation is developing heightened situational awareness. This goes beyond simple mindfulness—it's about cultivating a sophisticated understanding of context and consequences.

During my own recovery journey, I had to learn to read situations with new eyes. The same skills that once helped me detect threats on the football field had to be repurposed for detecting opportunities for growth and potential pitfalls in recovery. At Elevate, we teach this through structured observation exercises:

- Environmental scanning becomes a daily practice, where residents learn to notice not just obvious triggers but subtle environmental cues that might impact their recovery. This might mean recognizing how different social situations affect their emotional state, or understanding how physical environments influence their thought patterns.

- Interpersonal dynamics awareness develops through guided group interactions. Residents learn to notice how different relationship patterns affect their stability and growth. This awareness becomes crucial in maintaining recovery while rebuilding family relationships and professional connections.
- Internal state monitoring teaches the subtle art of tracking one's own psychological and emotional weather patterns. This isn't just about recognizing when you're stressed or triggered; it's about understanding the gradual build-up of pressure and taking preemptive action to maintain stability.

1. The Adaptation Cycle

Through years of observation and refinement, we've identified what we call the Adaptation Cycle—a recurring pattern that characterizes successful navigation of change. Understanding this cycle helps individuals and organizations move through change more effectively.

Recognition Phase

The cycle begins with recognition—not just of the need for change, but of the current reality in all its complexity. This means developing the capacity to see situations clearly, without the distortions of denial or wishful thinking.

During our businesses' early days, this meant honestly assessing both our capabilities and limitations. We had to recognize not just what we wanted to achieve, but what we could realistically accomplish with our resources. This honest assessment prevented us from overextending while identifying areas where we needed to build capacity.

Response Development

Once we clearly see our situation, the next phase involves developing appropriate responses. This isn't about quick reactions; it's about thoughtful, strategic adaptation that considers both immediate needs and long-term implications.

The response development phase involves several key elements:

- Strategic assessment requires evaluating multiple possible approaches and their potential outcomes. In our programs, we learned to consider not just the immediate impact of program changes, but their ripple effects through our entire community.
- Resource alignment means ensuring that our responses match our available resources—both tangible and intangible. This includes everything from staff capacity to community goodwill.
- Sustainability planning focuses on ensuring that our adaptations can be maintained over time. Short-term solutions often create long-term problems, so we learned to prioritize sustainable approaches even when they require more initial effort.

Implementation Intelligence

The way we implement change matters as much as the changes themselves. Implementation intelligence means understanding how to introduce adaptations in ways that promote acceptance and integration.

Timing becomes crucial—knowing when to push forward and when to allow time for integration. During our expansion phases, we learned that rushing implementation often created resistance that could have been avoided with better timing.

Pacing requires understanding the absorption capacity of individuals and systems. Just as in physical training, adaptation requires appropriate loading—too much too soon leads to rejection, while too little produces no growth.

Feedback integration means creating robust systems for gathering and responding to information about how changes are affecting all stakeholders. This isn't just about formal feedback mechanisms; it's about developing sensitive "listening posts" throughout the organization.

The Role of Leadership in Conscious Adaptation

Leadership during periods of adaptation requires a unique set of skills and awareness. Through building and growing my businesses, I've learned that adaptive leadership involves several crucial elements:

1. Embodied Learning

Leaders must model the adaptation they wish to see in others. This means actively engaging in our own growth and development while guiding others through change. During challenging periods at Elevate and True North, I found that my own adaptation journey became a powerful teaching tool for both staff and residents.

1. Strategic Patience

Understanding the natural rhythms of adaptation helps leaders maintain appropriate patience during change processes. This doesn't mean being passive; it means recognizing that meaningful change often requires time for integration and adjustment.

1. Dynamic Balance

Perhaps the most crucial skill in adaptive leadership is maintaining dynamic balance—keeping organizational stability while facilitating necessary change. This involves:

- Holding space for both stability and change, creating environments where people feel secure enough to take risks and try new approaches.
- Building trust through consistent demonstration of both commitment to mission and willingness to adapt methods as needed.
- Fostering innovation by encouraging experimentation within appropriate boundaries.

Measuring Adaptation Success

The effectiveness of conscious adaptation can be measured through various lenses:

Quantitative Metrics

- Retention rates in programs
- Achievement of adaptation goals
- Resource efficiency in change processes
- Success rates in new initiatives

Qualitative Indicators

- Individual growth stories
- Community feedback
- Organizational culture shifts
- Stakeholder satisfaction

Long-Term Impact

- Sustainable behavior change
- Program evolution
- Community integration
- Organizational resilience

Through these measurements, we continue to refine our under-standing and practice of conscious adaptation, creating ever more effective approaches to navigating change while maintaining core stability.

Advanced Applications of Conscious Adaptation

As our understanding of adaptation has deepened through years of work in the behavioral health field, we've discovered increas-ingly sophisticated applications of these principles across different contexts and challenges.

Crisis Navigation

Perhaps the most demanding test of conscious adaptation comes during times of crisis. Whether facing personal setbacks, organiza-tional challenges, or community resistance, the principles of conscious adaptation become essential survival tools.

During the height of our zoning battles, we faced a particularly difficult period where it seemed our entire project might collapse. Multiple residents needed to be temporarily relocated, funding was uncertain, and community opposition had reached a fever pitch. This situation demanded every aspect of conscious adapta-tion we had developed.

The first element was maintaining clarity despite the chaos. Rather than becoming reactive to each new challenge, we maintained our centered awareness, carefully assessing each situation before responding. This meant gathering our leadership team daily, sometimes hourly, to evaluate new developments and adjust our approach while keeping our core mission intact.

Our response integrated multiple levels of adaptation:

- Immediate crisis management required quick, decisive action to ensure resident safety and program continuity. We developed temporary housing partnerships with allied organizations while maintaining our support services through alternative venues.
- Strategic repositioning involved reassessing our community approach entirely. Rather than fighting opposition directly, we began hosting community education events and facilitating dialogue between residents and neighbors. This transformed many opponents into advocates as they began to understand the true nature of recovery and its benefit to the community.
- Long-term sustainability planning emerged from the crisis stronger than before. We developed more robust systems for community integration, crisis response, and program adaptation that continue to serve us today.

Organizational Evolution

The principles of conscious adaptation have profoundly influenced how we approach organizational development in my businesses. Rather than following rigid strategic plans, we've developed what we call "adaptive strategy"—an approach that maintains clear direction while remaining flexible in execution.

This manifests in several key ways:

1. Fluid Hierarchy

We've moved beyond traditional organizational structures to create what we call a "fluid hierarchy." While clear leadership and accountability remain essential, we've developed systems that allow expertise and responsibility to flow where needed based on circumstances and capabilities.

This approach has proven particularly valuable during rapid growth phases, where traditional hierarchies often become bottlenecks. Instead, we've created adaptive teams that can reconfigure based on current challenges while maintaining organizational coherence.

1. Learning Integration

Perhaps the most powerful aspect of organizational adaptation has been our approach to learning integration. Rather than periodic training sessions or annual reviews, we've developed continuous learning systems that allow real-time adaptation based on emerging insights and challenges.

This includes:

- Daily integration sessions where teams share insights and adjust approaches based on immediate feedback and experiences.
- Weekly pattern recognition meetings where we analyze emerging trends and adapt programs accordingly.
- Monthly strategic reviews that ensure our adaptations align with our core mission and values while meeting current needs.

Personal Evolution

Through all of this organizational and programmatic development, I've discovered that conscious adaptation is, at its core, a deeply personal practice. The same principles that guide organizational change prove invaluable in personal growth and development.

My own journey from athlete to inmate to recovery advocate has been a constant exercise in conscious adaptation. Each transition required not just external changes but deep internal transformation. This personal experience informs how we approach adaptation at every level of our organization.

The Future of Adaptation

As we look toward the future, the importance of conscious adaptation only grows. In an increasingly complex and rapidly changing world, the ability to adapt while maintaining core stability becomes not just beneficial but essential for survival and growth.

We continue to explore new frontiers in adaptive practice:

- Integration of technology tools that support adaptive processes while maintaining human connection at the center of our work.
- Development of more sophisticated feedback systems that allow for faster, more nuanced adaptation to changing needs.
- Expansion of our understanding of how different individuals and groups navigate change, allowing for more personalized support in adaptation processes.

Final Thoughts on Conscious Adaptation

The practice of conscious adaptation represents a fundamental shift in how we approach change and stability. Rather than seeing them as opposing forces, we recognize them as complementary aspects of healthy growth and development.

Through this lens, every challenge becomes an opportunity for refinement and growth. Every setback offers insights that strengthen our adaptive capacity. Every success provides lessons that can be integrated into our evolving understanding of how to navigate change effectively.

As you continue your own journey of growth and development, remember that conscious adaptation isn't about perfection; it's about progress. It's about developing the capacity to move through change with grace and purpose, maintaining your core stability while remaining open to the endless possibilities for growth and transformation that life presents.

The future belongs to those who can adapt consciously, maintaining their essential nature while evolving in response to changing circumstances. This is the art and science of conscious adaptation—a practice that continues to evolve as we discover new ways to navigate the ever-changing landscape of human experience.

10

A RESILIENT LIFE—BUILDING RESILIENCE AS A DAILY PRACTICE

Every morning, while the world still sleeps, I create a space of stillness in the pre-dawn quiet. This isn't some elaborate ritual—just a few precious minutes of meditation, clearing yesterday's noise and grounding myself in the present moment. The house is quiet, the day's demands haven't yet begun, and in this space, I find my center. It's nothing fancy—just me, my breath, and the growing awareness of a new day's possibilities.

This simple practice represents far more than just starting the day right. It's the foundation of what I've come to understand about sustainable resilience: It's not a resource you tap into during crisis, but a way of living that shapes every moment, every decision, and every interaction.

Creating a Resilient Lifestyle

The journey to sustainable resilience begins long before the sun rises. In those early morning hours, when the world is still dark and quiet, I've found something precious—a clarity that can't be replicated once the day's chaos begins. This isn't about being a morning person or following some productivity guru's advice. It's about creating space for what matters most.

My routine starts with meditation—just a few minutes to clear my mind and let go of any residual noise from yesterday. This quiet space becomes crucial for what follows. It's here, in these moments of stillness, that I set the foundation for the day ahead. Not by planning or strategizing, but by simply being present, allowing my mind to settle into a state of calm readiness.

After meditation, I dive straight into work. These early morning hours offer a unique kind of focus—no phone calls, no emails, no interruptions. Whether I'm tackling a major project for one of my businesses or planning our next community initiative, this time becomes a sacred space for focused effort. The goal isn't to chase results but to engage fully with the work itself, trusting that consistent effort will yield the right outcomes.

This approach to starting the day wasn't always natural. Like many habits worth building, it took time to develop. The key wasn't in forcing myself to become something I wasn't, but in recognizing the value of these quiet morning hours and gradually building a routine that honored them. Now, when my daughter wakes up, I'm present and centered, not already lost in the day's demands.

The practice of resilience extends far beyond these morning hours, though. Throughout the day, it shows up in countless small decisions: how to respond to unexpected challenges, when to push forward and when to pause, and how to maintain focus amid distractions. Each choice becomes an opportunity to strengthen the resilient foundation we're building.

Training for an Ironman while running these businesses and being present for my family isn't about superhuman time management; it's about integration. Each element supports the others, creating a synergy that would be impossible if they were treated as separate compartments of life. The physical discipline of training enhances mental clarity for work. The emotional demands of supporting others in recovery deepen my appreciation for family time. Everything connects, and everything contributes to building a more resilient whole.

The Mind-Body-Spirit Connection in Resilience

Sometimes, when life's weight becomes too heavy, I find myself drawn to the outdoors. It doesn't matter if it's a challenging mountain trail or just a quiet walk around the neighborhood—there's something about being outside that resets everything. The fresh air, the open space, the simple act of moving through nature—it all works together to clear the mental clutter that accumulates through daily life.

I've learned that you don't need epic landscapes to find this connection. While the mountains offer their own profound lessons, even a brief walk down a city street or a few minutes on a park bench can provide the space needed to reconnect with yourself. Nature, in whatever form you find it, has this remarkable way of putting things in perspective.

During these outdoor moments, whether I'm training for an event or just taking a mindful walk, the boundary between physical and spiritual practice often dissolves. The rhythmic movement of running, the steady cadence of breathing, the feeling of wind against your face—it all becomes a form of moving meditation. This is where Buddhism and athletics merge in my practice, where physical training becomes spiritual growth.

The Buddhist teachings I encountered have profoundly shaped how I approach both athletic training and daily life. It's not about achieving some state of enlightenment or breaking physical records; it's about being present with whatever's happening, whether that's the burn in your muscles during a hard workout or the emotional weight of a challenging day in the office.

This integration of physical and spiritual practice has taught me that resilience isn't compartmentalized. You can't be physically resilient while emotionally fragile, or spiritually centered while physically neglected. Everything connects, and everything contributes to your overall capacity for resilience.

The lessons from Buddhism complement rather than conflict with athletic training. Both require discipline, presence, and nonattachment to outcomes. When I'm out on a long training run, these principles come alive. Each step becomes an opportunity to practice presence. Each moment of discomfort becomes a chance to observe without judgment. Each mile becomes a lesson in impermanence—everything changes, everything passes, everything flows.

Fostering a Resilient Community

The Active Recovery Community we've built together represents something far more powerful than just a group workout session. Every time we come together—whether it's for a challenging bike ride, a climbing session, a run, or even a simple game of frisbee golf—we're building something larger than individual fitness goals. We're creating a space where resilience grows through connection, and where strength multiplies through sharing.

Competition runs deep in our community's DNA, but it's not about tearing each other down. It's about that spark of friendly rivalry that pushes everyone to discover their true capabilities. When we're out there sweating together, pushing through fatigue, or breaking through perceived limitations, we're demonstrating that resilience grows stronger in the community.

The beauty of this approach lies in its variety. One week we might be tackling a challenging hike, the next we're engaged in an intense game of pickleball, and the following week we're doing group workouts in the park. This constant variation isn't random; it's intentional. It teaches adaptability, prevents stagnation, and keeps everyone engaged and growing.

What makes this community special isn't just the physical challenges we share. It's the way we celebrate each other's progress, support each other through setbacks, and create an environment where everyone feels pushed to grow while remaining completely supported. Every personal best, every milestone reached, every small victory becomes a collective celebration.

The principles we practice in our active recovery sessions translate directly into daily life. The mental toughness developed during a challenging workout becomes emotional resilience during difficult conversations. The support we offer each other during physical challenges becomes the foundation for deeper connections in all areas of life.

This community approach to resilience has taught me something crucial: Strength multiplies when shared. When someone in our group breaks through a barrier—whether it's completing their first unassisted pull-up or running their longest distance—it creates a ripple effect. Others begin to question their own limitations, to push beyond their comfort zones, to discover capabilities they didn't know they possessed.

The impact extends far beyond physical fitness. Members of our community often report that the confidence gained through our shared challenges carries over into their professional lives, their relationships, and their recovery journeys. This is because true resilience, once developed, doesn't remain confined to one area of life—it infuses everything you do.

Building Sustainable Practice

Creating a resilient life isn't about occasional heroic efforts; it's about consistent, sustainable practices that become as natural as breathing. The morning meditation that grounds my day, the community workouts that build collective strength, the quiet moments in nature that restore perspective—these aren't separate activities. They're interconnected elements of a lifestyle designed to foster resilience.

The key to sustainability lies in integration rather than addition. Instead of trying to squeeze new practices into an already full life, we look for ways to enhance what we're already doing. A commute becomes an opportunity for mindfulness. A family walk becomes a chance to connect with nature. A work challenge becomes an opportunity to practice emotional resilience.

This approach to building resilience requires patience and consistency. Just as you can't build physical strength through sporadic, intense workouts, you can't develop lasting resilience through occasional practices. It's the daily choices, the small moments of mindful attention, the consistent showing up that creates lasting change.

Deepening the Practice

The sustainability of resilient living extends far beyond basic routines and practices. Through years of working with recovery communities and developing my own practice, I've discovered layers of depth that continue to reveal themselves.

The Rhythm of Resilient Living

Sustainable resilience follows natural rhythms—daily cycles, seasonal changes, and life transitions. Each of these rhythms offers unique opportunities for deepening our practice. During winter months, for example, our Active Recovery Community adapts our outdoor activities to embrace the challenge of cold weather training. These adaptations aren't just about maintaining fitness; they teach valuable lessons about flexibility and perseverance.

The daily rhythm begins with those pre-dawn hours of stillness, but it doesn't end there. Throughout the day, we find moments to reset and reconnect. A brief meditation between meetings, a mindful walk during lunch break, or a few minutes of focused breathing before an important conversation—these micro-practices maintain our resilient foundation.

The Role of Rest in Resilience

One of the most counterintuitive lessons I've learned about sustainable resilience is the crucial role of rest. Not just physical rest, but mental and emotional restoration as well. In our Active Recovery Community, we've instituted what we call "restoration days"—dedicated times when we focus on gentle movement, meditation, and community connection rather than intense physical challenges.

These aren't just rest days in the traditional sense. They're opportunities to practice different aspects of resilience:

- Deep listening to our bodies and minds
- Strengthening social bonds through unhurried conversation
- Practicing the art of being present without the drive to achieve

Advanced Integration Practices

As our community has evolved, we've developed more sophisticated approaches to integrating different aspects of resilience practice. For instance, we've created what we call "mindful challenge sessions" where physical training becomes a laboratory for practicing presence and emotional regulation.

During these sessions, participants might engage in challenging physical tasks while maintaining complete awareness of their thought patterns and emotional responses. This integration of physical challenge with mental awareness creates powerful opportunities for growth and insight.

The Ecology of Resilience

Understanding resilience as an ecological system has transformed how we approach practice. Every element—physical training, meditation, community connection, nature exposure—influences and supports the others. This systems thinking helps us create more effective and sustainable practices.

For example, we've noticed how time spent in nature enhances both physical recovery and emotional well-being. This has led us to intentionally incorporate outdoor elements into our recovery programs, even in urban settings. Something as simple as maintaining a community garden provides multiple benefits:

- Physical activity through gardening

- Connection with natural cycles
- Community building through shared work
- Mindfulness practice through focused attention
- Nutritional benefits from fresh produce

Technology and Resilience

While our practice emphasizes natural rhythms and direct experience, we've also found ways to thoughtfully incorporate technology to support sustainable resilience. Mobile apps for meditation tracking, community platforms for coordinating activities, and wearable devices for monitoring recovery—these tools can enhance rather than replace fundamental practices.

The key is maintaining technology as a servant rather than a master. We use digital tools to support our practice while ensuring they don't become distractions from direct experience and genuine connection.

Cultivating Resilient Leadership

Sustainable resilience requires effective leadership—not just from designated leaders but from everyone in the community. We've developed what we call "distributed resilience leadership," where different community members step forward to share their strengths and insights.

This approach creates multiple benefits:

- Broader ownership of community well-being
- More diverse perspectives on resilience practice
- Increased sustainability through shared responsibility
- Enhanced learning through peer teaching and mentoring

The Art of Sustainable Growth

Perhaps the most sophisticated aspect of sustainable resilience is understanding how to foster growth without creating burnout. This requires careful attention to the balance between challenge and recovery, between individual development and community support.

We've learned to recognize the signs of unsustainable practice:

- Decreased engagement in community activities
- Loss of joy in physical training
- Rigid adherence to routines without flexibility
- Diminished presence in daily activities

By staying attuned to these indicators, we can adjust our practices to maintain sustainable growth over the long term.

Looking Forward

The journey of building sustainable resilience never truly ends. As our understanding deepens and our community grows, we continue to discover new dimensions of practice. The key is maintaining our commitment to growth while honoring the fundamental principles that support lasting resilience.

The future holds exciting possibilities for expanding our understanding and practice of sustainable resilience. Whether through new scientific insights into the mind-body connection, innovative approaches to community building, or a deeper understanding of how nature supports human well-being, we remain open to evolution while staying grounded in proven principles.

Remember that sustainable resilience isn't about reaching a destination; it's about creating a way of living that supports continuous growth and adaptation. Through consistent practice, community support, and mindful attention to all aspects of well-being, we build not just individual strength but collective resilience that can weather any storm.

This is your practice now. Make it count. Every morning meditation, every shared workout, every moment of connection becomes part of building a more resilient future—not just for yourself, but for everyone your life touches.

AFTERWORD

There's a moment I'll never forget. It was early morning at one of our Elevate Homes, and one of our residents—let's call him Mike —was sitting across from me, his eyes filled with a familiar mix of desperation and defeat. "I can't do this," he said, his voice barely above a whisper. "I'm not strong enough." Looking at him, I saw myself years ago, sitting in that same place of hopelessness, believing the same lies about my own capabilities.

What happened next wasn't about giving advice or offering empty encouragement. It was about sharing the truth I'd learned through my own journey: Resilience isn't about being strong enough; it's about being willing to take the next step, even when you don't feel strong at all. That conversation with Mike became a turning point, not just for him but for my understanding of what resilience really means.

The Circle of Resilience

One of the most profound lessons I've learned is that resilience doesn't reach its full potential until it's shared. Every triumph over adversity, every lesson learned through struggle, every insight gained through experience—these aren't just personal victories. They're tools that can help others find their way through their own challenges.

I see pieces of my own story in every person I work with in our programs. Some are where I was during those dark days of addiction, feeling trapped and hopeless. Others are like I was in early recovery, taking their first tentative steps toward a new life. Still, others remind me of myself during the challenges of building these businesses, facing uncertainty and self-doubt while trying to create something meaningful.

Each interaction becomes an opportunity to share not just what I've learned, but what I'm still learning. Because here's the truth about resilience: It's not a destination you reach once and then stop. It's an ongoing journey of growth, discovery, and evolution. Every new challenge brings fresh lessons, and every setback offers new insights to share.

The Power of Authentic Connection

Mentoring others has taught me that the most powerful tool in building resilience isn't advice or instruction; it's authentic connection. When I share my own struggles, doubts, and failures, it creates space for others to be honest about theirs. This raw authenticity breaks down the barriers that often prevent people from embracing their own capacity for resilience.

I remember working with a former athlete who was struggling in recovery. Like me, he'd built his identity around being strong, being unbeatable. Sharing my own journey of learning that true strength often means admitting weakness helped him begin to see his situation differently. It wasn't about giving up his identity as an athlete; it was about expanding it to include new kinds of strength.

This kind of mentoring isn't about having all the answers. It's about walking alongside someone as they discover their own path to resilience. Sometimes that means sharing specific techniques or strategies. Other times it means simply being present, offering the kind of understanding that only comes from having walked a similar path.

Investment in Growth

True mentorship goes beyond occasional conversations or sporadic advice. It's about investing in someone else's journey, being there for the victories and the setbacks, the breakthroughs and the struggles. This investment isn't just about time; it's about emotional presence, genuine care, and unwavering belief in some-one's potential, even when they can't see it themselves.

At Elevate, True North, and All The Way Well, we've created a culture where this kind of investment is the norm. Whether it's in our recovery programs, our active community events, or our day-to-day interactions, we're constantly looking for ways to help others build their resilience. This isn't about creating dependency; it's about empowering people to discover their own strength while knowing they have support when they need it.

The impact of this approach ripples out far beyond individual success stories. When someone discovers their capacity for resilience and then shares that discovery with others, it creates a chain reaction of growth and empowerment. I've watched people who once doubted their ability to stay sober become powerful mentors to others in early recovery. I've seen people who thought they could never achieve their goals become inspirations for others facing similar challenges.

The Evolution of Teaching

As my own journey has evolved, so has my approach to helping others build resilience. Early on, I focused mainly on sharing specific techniques and strategies—the same ones that had helped me in my recovery and personal growth. While these practical tools are important, I've learned that the most powerful teaching comes through example.

Living resilience daily, facing challenges openly, admitting mistakes, and continuously growing—these actions speak louder than any advice I could give. When people see authentic resilience in action, it helps them believe in their own capacity for growth and change.

This evolution in teaching has also meant learning to meet people where they are. Everyone's path to resilience is unique, shaped by their own experiences, challenges, and strengths. What works for one person might not work for another. The key is helping each individual discover their own way while providing the support and guidance they need to keep moving forward.

Creating Lasting Impact

The true measure of resilience isn't just personal success; it's the impact we have on others. Every person who finds their strength and goes on to help others creates a ripple effect that can transform communities. This is how resilience becomes more than individual achievement; it becomes a force for collective growth and positive change.

At Elevate, True North, and All The Way Well, we see this ripple effect in action every day. Former residents return to share their stories, mentor others, and contribute to the community that helped them find their way. Each success story becomes an inspiration for others still struggling, and each person who discovers their resilience becomes a potential mentor for someone else.

This approach to building resilience creates something sustainable—a continuous cycle of growth, support, and empowerment that strengthens individuals and communities alike. It's not about creating dependency or positioning ourselves as saviors. It's about fostering an environment where everyone has the opportunity to both receive and offer support.

The Legacy of Resilience

As I reflect on my journey from addiction to recovery, from struggle to strength, from being mentored to mentoring others, I'm struck by how the meaning of resilience has evolved for me. What started as a personal quest for survival has become something much larger—a mission to help others discover their own capacity for growth and transformation.

The legacy I hope to leave isn't just about the lives I've personally touched or the organizations I've built. It's about creating a ripple effect of resilience that continues long after I'm gone. Every person who discovers their strength and goes on to help others adds to this legacy, creating an ever-expanding circle of impact.

This is why I wrote this book—not just to share my story or teach specific techniques, but to inspire others to discover their own resilience and then share it with others. The principles and practices we've explored aren't meant to be followed exactly as written.

They're starting points for your own journey of discovery, your own path to building and sharing resilience.

Looking Forward

As you close this book and continue on your own journey, remember that resilience isn't a destination; it's a continuous process of growth, learning, and sharing. Your struggles, your victories, your insights, and your experiences all have value, not just for your own development but for others who might benefit from your story.

Don't be afraid to share your journey with others. Your vulnerability might be exactly what someone else needs to find their strength. Your setbacks might help someone else persist through difficulty. Your victories might inspire someone else to keep going when they want to quit.

Remember too that seeking support isn't a sign of weakness; it's a demonstration of wisdom. None of us becomes resilient in isolation. We grow stronger through connection, sharing, supporting, and being supported by others.

Most importantly, know that wherever you are in your journey—whether you're just beginning to build resilience or you're already helping others find their way—you have something valuable to contribute. Your experiences, your insights, and your presence can make a difference in someone else's life.

This is the ultimate purpose of resilience: not just to overcome our own challenges, but to help others discover their capacity to do the same. In doing so, we create something larger than ourselves—a legacy of strength, growth, and positive change that continues to impact lives long after our own journey ends.

As you move forward from these pages, carry with you the knowledge that you're not just building resilience for yourself; you're becoming part of a larger story of transformation and growth. Your journey matters, not just for what it means to you, but for how it might inspire and encourage others.

This is your opportunity to become part of the circle of resilience —to receive support when you need it and to offer it when you can. In doing so, you'll discover that the true power of resilience lies not just in what it helps us overcome, but in what it enables us to create together.

Make your journey count. Share your strength. Pass it on.

BIBLIOGRAPHY

Arida, R. M., & Teixeira-Machado, L. (2021). The contribution of physical exercise to brain resilience. *App.dimensions.ai*, *14*(626769). https://doi.org/10.3389/fnbeh.2020.626769

Bolouki, A. (2022). Neurobiological effects of urban built and natural environment on mental health: systematic review. *Reviews on Environmental Health*, *0*(0). https://doi.org/10.1515/reveh-2021-0137

Chodavadia, P., Teo, I., Poremski, D., Fung, D. S. S., & Finkelstein, E. A. (2023). Prevalence and economic burden of depression and anxiety symptoms among Singaporean adults: results from a 2022 web panel. *BMC Psychiatry*, *23*(1). https://doi.org/10.1186/s12888-023-04581-7

Li, F., Luo, S., Mu, W., Li, Y., Ye, L., Zheng, X., Xu, B., Ding, Y., Ling, P., Zhou, M., & Chen, X. (2021). Effects of sources of social support and resilience on the mental health of different age groups during the COVID-19 pandemic. *BMC Psychiatry*, *21*(1), 1–14. https://doi.org/10.1186/s12888-020-03012-1

Lin, Y., & Feng, T. (2024). Lateralization of self-control over the dorsolateral prefrontal cortex in decision-making: a systematic review and meta-analytic evidence from noninvasive brain stimulation. *Cognitive, Affective, & Behavioral Neuroscience*. https://doi.org/10.3758/s13415-023-01148-7

Manjula, M., & Srivastava, A. K. (2022). *Resilience: Concepts, approaches, indicators, and interventions for sustainability of positive mental health*. 607–636. https://doi.org/10.1007/978-981-16-8263-6_26

McGaffin, B. J., Deane, F. P., Kelly, P. J., & Blackman, R. J. (2017). Social support and mental health during recovery from drug and alcohol problems. *Addiction Research & Theory*, *26*(5), 386–395. https://doi.org/10.1080/16066359.2017.1421178

NeuroLaunch editorial team. (2024, September 15). *Environment in psychology: Defining its role in human behavior and development*. NeuroLaunch.com. https://neurolaunch.com/environment-definition-psychology/

Ozbay, F., Johnson, D. C., Dimoulas, E., Morgan, C., Charney, D., & Southwick, S. (2007). Social support and resilience to stress: From neurobiology to clinical practice. *Psychiatry (Edgmont)*, *4*(5), 35. https://pmc.ncbi.nlm.nih.gov/articles/PMC2921311/

Sagone, E., Commodari, E., Indiana, M. L., & La Rosa, V. L. (2023). Exploring the association between attachment style, psychological well-being, and relationship status in young adults and adults—a cross-sectional study. *European Journal of*

Investigation in Health, Psychology and Education, 13(3), 525–539. https://doi.org/10. 3390/ejihpe13030040

Stein, M. (2023). *For relationship maintenance, accurate perception of partner's behavior is key | College of Agricultural, Consumer & Environmental Sciences | Illinois.* Illinois.edu. https://aces.illinois.edu/news/relationship-maintenance-accurate-perception-partners-behavior-key

Sun, L. (2023). Social media usage and students' social anxiety, loneliness and wellbeing: Does digital mindfulness-based intervention effectively work? *BMC Psychology, 11*(1). https://doi.org/10.1186/s40359-023-01398-7

Vanden, P., Vandebosch, H., Koster, E. H. W., Tom De Leyn, Kyle Van Gaeveren, David, Sara Van Bruyssel, Tim van Timmeren, Lieven De Marez, Karolien Poels, DeSmet, A., Bram De Wever, Verbruggen, M., & Elfi Baillien. (2024). Why, how, when, and for whom does digital disconnection work? A process-based framework of digital disconnection. *Communication Theory.* https://doi.org/10.1093/ct/qtad016

Taylor, S. E. (2011). *Tend and Befriend Theory.* https://taylorlab.psych.ucla.edu/wp-content/uploads/sites/5/2014/11/2011_Tend-and-Befriend-Theory.pdf